Mountain Biking
Phoenix

BRUCE GRUBBS

FALCON® Helena, Montana

ᴀFALCONGUIDE®

Falcon® Publishing is continually expanding its list of recreational guide-books. All books include detailed descriptions, accurate maps, and all information necessary for enjoyable trips. You can order extra copies of this book and get information and prices for other Falcon® books by writing Falcon, P.O. Box 1718, Helena, Montana 59624 or calling toll free 1-800-582-2665. Also, please ask for a free copy of our current catalog. Visit our website at www.FalconOutdoors.com or contact us by e-mail at falcon@falcon.com

Project Editor: Peggy O'Neill-McLeod
Production Editor: Larissa Berry
Copyeditor: Kathryn McEnery
Page Compositor: SRC Graphics
Book and cover design by Falcon Publishing, Inc.

Cataloging-in-Publication data is on file at the Library of Congress.

CAUTION
Outdoor recreational activities are by their very nature potentially hazardous. All participants in such activities must assume responsibility for their own actions and safety. The information contained in this guidebook cannot replace sound judgment and good decision-making skills, which help reduce risk exposure, nor does the scope of this book allow for the disclosure of all the potential hazards and risks involved in such activities.

Learn as much as possible about the outdoor recreational activities in which you participate, prepare for the unexpected, and be cautious. The reward will be a safer and more enjoyable experience.

 Text pages printed on recycled paper.

Contents

Acknowledgments

I'd like to thank the following people for their help with this book. For reviewing the manuscript and providing many helpful suggestions, I owe thanks to the personnel of the Tonto National Forest, the Bureau of Land Management, the Maricopa County Parks and Recreation Department, and the Phoenix City Parks and Library Department. You're too numerous to mention but this book would not have been possible without you. Thanks to Jean Rukkila, experienced writer and outdoorswoman, for an excellent job of proofreading. Thanks to Art Christiansen both for giving me a place to crash and for valuable advice on riding in the Tonto National Forest, which is, after all, his backyard. And thanks to Doug and Kathy Rickard for another place to sleep in the Valley. Thanks to Bill Murphy, manager of the bike shop at Elk Meadows Resort, Utah, for keeping me on a rideable bike and for his valuable technical advice. We all owe a great deal of thanks to the individuals, groups, and agencies who build and maintain the trails. Thanks to editors John Burbidge and Peggy O'Neill-McLeod, and Larissa Berry, production editor, and all the other folks at Falcon Publishing who helped turn my manuscript into a finished book. This project would not have been possible without the encouragement and support, not to mention car shuttles, provided by Duart Martin.

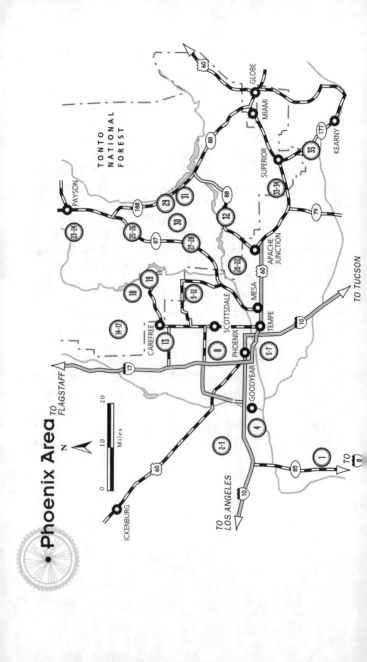

MAP LEGEND

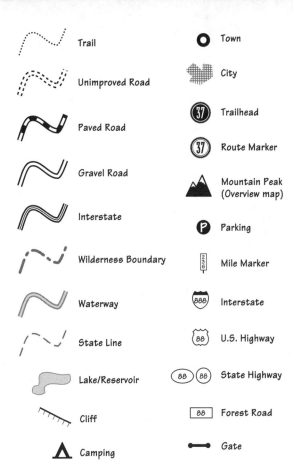

Trail

Unimproved Road

Paved Road

Gravel Road

Interstate

Wilderness Boundary

Waterway

State Line

Lake/Reservoir

Cliff

Camping

Ruins

Town

City

Trailhead

Route Marker

Mountain Peak
(Overview map)

Parking

Mile Marker

Interstate

U.S. Highway

State Highway

Forest Road

Gate

Building

Get Ready to Crank!

Where to ride? It's a quandary that faces every mountain biker, beginner or expert, local or tourist.

If you're new to the area, where do you start? If you're a long-time local, how do you avoid the rut of riding the same old trails week after week? And how do you find new terrain that's challenging but not overwhelming? Or an easier ride for when your not-so-serious buddies come along?

Welcome to *Mountain Biking Phoenix*. Here are 35 rides ranging from easy road routes to smooth singletrack to bravado-busting boulder fields. The rides are described in plain language, with accurate distances and ratings for physical and technical difficulty. Each entry offers a wealth of detailed information that's easy to read and use, from an armchair or on the trail.

My aim is threefold: to help you choose a ride that's appropriate for your fitness and skill level; to make it easy to find the trailhead; and to help you complete the ride safely, without getting lost. Take care of those basics and fun is bound to break loose.

The Phoenix Area: What to Expect

The rides in the Phoenix area cover a wide variety of terrain—from desert flats and mountains to forested mountain ridges. The trails can be steep and rough, and the weather—well, the record summer temperature in Phoenix is 122 degrees F. At high elevations summer thunderstorms are common, and snow falls in the winter.

Rugged terrain requires preparedness. Get in good shape before you attempt these rides, and know your limits. Clean and maintain your bike frequently. Before each ride, check tires, rims, brakes, handlebars, seat, shifters, derailleurs, and chain to make sure they survived the last ride and are functioning properly.

A helmet is essential for safe mountain biking; it can save your life and prevent serious injuries. Cycling gloves are another essential piece of safety equipment that can save hands from cuts and bruises from falls, encroaching branches, and rocks. They also improve your grip and comfort on the handlebars.

Always pack at least one (filled) water bottle, preferably two, or the equivalent. Rides in the Phoenix area are very hot in the summer and you'll want more water. A gallon is not too much on long, hot rides. A snack such as fruit or energy bars can keep those mighty thighs cranking for hours and prevent dreaded "bonk"—the sudden loss of energy when your body runs out of fuel. Dress for the weather and pack a wind- and water-proof jacket just in case, especially in the winter. The Arizona summer sun packs a wallop, even at higher altitudes where the air is cooler. Don't forget sunglasses, sunscreen, and lip balm. Insects can be a problem for a short period in the spring, especially in wet years. You may want to carry insect repellent.

It's wise to carry a small tool kit with appropriate tools for your bike, a spare tube, and a patch kit. A tire pump is a

2

must. You'll want to fill your tubes with leak repair goo; the desert is full of thorns and spines. Consider thicker, thorn-resistant tubes also.

This book is designed to be easily carried in a pocket or bike bag, and the maps and ride descriptions will help anyone unfamiliar with the trails. U.S. Geological Survey topographic maps can provide a more detailed view of the terrain, but ride routes may not be shown. The correct topo maps are listed for each ride. Some of the rides are on the Tonto National Forest; the USDA Forest Service map is useful for finding approach roads and some of the rides.

Finally, I'll say it again—always wear a helmet.

The **weather** in central Arizona's Sonoran desert spans the range of North American extremes. On the highest rides in the Mazatzal Mountains, snow is common from December through March. Summer highs routinely top 110 degrees F in the lower desert country. In general, higher elevations are cooler (by as much as 6 degrees F for every 1,000 feet) and windier. If you drive to a trailhead, play it safe and take a variety of clothes in the car to match the weather you're likely to encounter.

That said, we ride here year round. Most of the trails around Phoenix are best between October and April, but are also rideable early in the morning during the hot season. The higher elevation trails are best from April through November, though in dry years they can be ridden all winter. The best seasons overall are spring and fall. (Bear in mind that hunting seasons may occur during the good fall riding weather. Check with the Arizona Game & Fish Department for current hunting seasons. See the appendix. If you choose to ride where hunts are taking place, a blaze orange vest is a sensible precaution.)

Afternoon thunderstorms are common during July, August, and September. These storms often appear suddenly and can be severe, with hail, high wind, and lightning. If caught in a thunderstorm, get off high ridges and take shelter in a low-lying area or in a vehicle. Do not remain under lone trees. In the higher mountains during thunderstorm season, the mornings generally dawn sweet and clear, the air refreshed by yesterday's showers. Up here, it's a good idea to complete your day's riding by noon.

The rides in this book vary from 1,000 feet to more than 7,000 feet in elevation, which means you really can ride dirt all year, somewhere.

Please stay off wet, muddy trails—the soil damage and erosion one rider can cause is simply too great.

Rules of the Trail

If every mountain biker always yielded the right-of-way, stayed on the trail, avoided wet or muddy trails, never cut switchbacks, always rode in control, showed respect for other trail users, and carried out every last scrap of what was carried in (candy wrappers and bike-part debris included)—in short, if we all did the right thing—we wouldn't need a list of rules governing our behavior.

Fact is, most mountain bikers are conscientious and are trying to do the right thing. No one becomes good at something as demanding and painful as grunting up mountainsides by cheating.

Most of us don't need rules.

But we do need knowledge of what exactly is the right thing to do.

Here are some guidelines, reprinted by permission from the International Mountain Bicycling Association. The basic idea is to prevent or minimize damage to land, water, plants, and wildlife, and to avoid conflicts with other backcountry visitors and trail users. Ride with respect.

IMBA Rules of the Trail

Thousands of miles of dirt trails have been closed to mountain bicyclists. The irresponsible riding habits of a few riders have been a factor. Do your part to maintain trail access by observing the following rules of the trail, formulated by the International Mountain Bicycling Association (IMBA). IMBA's mission is to promote environmentally sound and socially responsible mountain biking.

1. Ride on open trails only. Respect trail and road closures (ask if not sure), avoid possible trespass on private land, obtain permits and authorization as may be required. Federal wilderness areas are closed to bicycles and all other mechanized and motorized equipment. The way you ride will influence trail management decisions and policies.

2. Leave no trace. Be sensitive to the dirt beneath you. Even on open (legal) trails, you should not ride under conditions where you will leave evidence of your passing, such as on certain soils after a rain. Recognize different types of soils and trail construction; practice low-impact cycling. This also means staying on existing trails and not creating new ones. Be sure to pack out at least as much as you pack in. Some of the rides feature optional side hikes into wilderness areas. Be a low impact hiker also.

3. Control your bicycle! Inattention for even a second can cause problems. Obey all bicycle speed regulations and recommendations.

4. Always yield trail. Make known your approach well in advance. A friendly greeting (or bell) is considerate and works well; don't startle others. Show your respect when passing by slowing to a walking pace or stopping. Anticipate other trail users at corners and blind spots.

5. Never spook animals. All animals are startled by an unannounced approach, a sudden movement, or a loud noise. This can be dangerous for you, others, and the animals. Give animals extra room and time to adjust to you. When passing horses, use special care and follow directions from the horseback riders (dismount and ask if uncertain). Chasing cattle and disturbing wildlife is a serious offense. Leave gates as you found them or as marked.

6. Plan ahead. Know your equipment, your ability, and the area in which you are riding—and prepare accordingly. Be self-sufficient at all times, keep your equipment in good repair, and carry necessary supplies for changes in weather or other conditions. A well-executed trip is a satisfaction to you and not a burden or offense to others. Always wear a helmet.

Keep trails open by setting a good example of environmentally sound and socially responsible off-road cycling.

How to Use this Guide

Mountain Biking Phoenix describes 35 mountain bike rides in their entirety.

Many of the featured rides are loops, beginning and ending at the same point but coming and going on different trails. Loops are by far the most popular type of ride, and we're lucky to have so many in the area.

Be forewarned, however: the difficulty of a loop may change dramatically depending on which direction you ride around the loop. If you are unfamiliar with the rides in this book, try them first as described here. The directions follow the path of least resistance and most fun (which does not necessarily mean easy). After you've been over the terrain, you can determine whether a given loop would be fun—or even feasible—in the reverse direction. Some trails are designated as one way, so you don't have a choice.

Portions of some rides follow maintained dirt or even paved roads. A word about desert dirt roads: because the weather is so stable and dry much of the year, many dirt roads, though officially maintained, don't actually receive much attention. The surface may become loose because of accumulating sand and gravel, and washboarded roads can be a pain.

Each ride description follows the same format:

Number: Each ride is numbered, both in the description and the table of contents.

Name: For the most part, I relied on official names of trails, roads, and natural features as shown on USDA Forest Service and U.S. Geological Survey maps. In some cases deference was given to long-term local custom.

Location: Direction and approximate distance from Phoenix or the nearest of its satellite cities. Exact distances are not given because the urban area is so large.

Distance: The length of the ride in miles, given as a loop, one way (if shuttled), or out and back.

7

Time: A conservative estimate of how long it takes to complete the ride—for example: 1 to 2 hours. *The time listed is the actual riding time and does not include rest stops.* Strong, skilled riders may be able to do a given ride in less than the estimated time, while other riders may take considerably longer. Also bear in mind that severe weather, changes in trail conditions, or mechanical problems may prolong a ride.

Tread: The type of road or trail—paved road, maintained dirt road, doubletrack, or singletrack.

Aerobic level: The level of physical effort required to complete the ride: Easy, moderate, or strenuous as described below:

Easy: Flat or gently rolling terrain, with no steep or prolonged climbs.

Moderate: Some hills: the climbs may be short and fairly steep, or long and gradual. There may be short hills that less fit riders will want to walk.

Strenuous: Frequent or prolonged climbs steep enough to require riding in the lowest gear; requires a high level of aerobic fitness, power, and endurance (typically acquired through many hours of riding and proper training). Less fit riders may need to walk.

Many rides are mostly easy and moderate but may have short strenuous sections. Other rides are mostly strenuous and should be attempted only after a complete medical checkup and implant of a second heart, preferably a big one. Also be aware that flailing through a highly technical section can be exhausting even on the flats. Good riding skills and a relaxed stance on the bike save energy.

Finally, any ride can be strenuous if you ride it hard and fast. Conversely, the pain of a lung-burning climb grows easier to tolerate as your fitness level improves. Learn to pace yourself and remember to schedule easy rides and rest days into your calendar.

Technical difficulty: The level of bike-handling skills needed to complete the ride upright and in one piece. Technical difficulty is rated on a scale of 1 to 5, with 1 being the easiest and 5 the hardest. These are described below.

Level 1: Smooth tread; road or doubletrack; no obstacles, ruts, or steep climbs. Requires basic bike-handling skills.

Level 2: Mostly smooth tread; wide, well-groomed singletrack or road/doubletrack with minor ruts or loose gravel or sand.

Level 3: Irregular tread with some rough sections; slickrock, single or doubletrack with obvious route choices; some steep sections; occasional obstacles may include small rocks, roots, water bars, ruts, loose gravel or sand, and sharp turns or broad, open switchbacks.

Level 4: Rough tread with few smooth places; singletrack or rough doubletrack with limited route choices; steep sections, some with obstacles; obstacles are numerous and varied, including rocks, roots, branches, ruts, sidehills, narrow tread, loose gravel or sand, and switchbacks. Most slickrock falls in this level.

Level 5: Continuously broken, rocky, root-infested, or trenched tread; singletrack or extremely rough doubletrack with few route choices; frequent, sudden, and severe changes in gradient; some slopes so steep that wheels lift off ground; obstacles are nearly continuous and may include boulders, logs, water, large holes, deep ruts, ledges, piles of loose gravel, steep sidehills, encroaching trees, and tight switchbacks.

I've also added plus (+) and minus (-) symbols to cover gray areas between given levels of difficulty; a 4+ obstacle is harder than a 4, but easier than a -5. A stretch of trail rated 5+ would be unrideable by all but the most skilled riders.

Again, most of the rides in this book cover varied terrain, with an ever-changing degree of technical difficulty. Some trails run smooth with only occasional obstacles, and other trails are seemingly all obstacles. The path of least resistance, or line, is where you find it. In general, most obstacles are more challenging if you encounter them while climbing than while descending. On the other hand, in heavy surf (e.g., boulder fields, tangles of downfall, cliffs), fear plays a larger role when facing downhill.

Understand that different riders have different strengths and weaknesses. Some folks can scramble over logs and boulders without a grunt, but they crash head over heels on every switchback turn. Some fly off the steepest slopes and others freeze. Some riders climb like the wind and others just blow and walk.

The key to overcoming technical difficulties is practice: keep trying. Follow a rider who makes it look easy, and don't hesitate to ask for constructive criticism. Try shifting your weight (good riders move a lot, front to back, side to side, and up and down) and experimenting with balance and momentum. Find a smooth patch of lawn and practice riding as slowly as possible, even balancing in a track stand (described in the glossary). This will give you more confidence—and more time to recover or bail out—the next time the trail rears up and bites.

Hazards: A list of dangers that may be encountered on a ride, including traffic, weather, trail obstacles and conditions, risky stream crossings, obscure trails, and other perils. Remember: conditions may change at any time. Be alert for storms, new fences, deadfall, missing trail signs, and mechanical failure. Fatigue, heat, cold, and/or dehydration may impair judgment. Always wear a helmet and other safety equipment. Ride in control at all times. If a section of trail seems too difficult for you, it's cool to get off and walk your bike through the bad section.

Highlights: Special features or qualities that make a ride worth doing (as if we needed an excuse!): scenery, fun singletrack, chances to see wildlife.

Land status: A list of managing agencies or landowners. Most of the rides in this book are on public land belonging to one of the cities, Maricopa County, or Tonto National Forest. But many of the rides also cross portions of private lands. Always leave gates as you found them or as signed. And respect the land and property, regardless of who owns it. Because the Phoenix area is growing so rapidly, I left out some popular rides that are on land threatened by development. See the appendix for a list of USDA Forest Service addresses.

Maps: A list of available maps. The Tonto National Forest map at a scale of 1:126,720 affords a good overview of travel routes and some of the rides in the New River Mountains, Mazatzal Mountains, and Superstition Mountains. The Arizona Atlas published by DeLorme Mapping at a scale of 1:250,000 gives a good topographic overview. USGS topographic maps in the 7.5-minute series give a close-up look at terrain. Not all routes are shown on official maps. Most of the city and county parks have trail maps; see the appendix for contact information.

Access: How to find the trailhead or the start of the ride, starting from a major street or highway in Phoenix or the nearest of its satellite cities. If you're lucky enough to live near one of the rides, you may be able to pedal to the start. For most riders, it'll be necessary to drive to the trailhead.

The ride: A mile-by-mile list of key points—landmarks, notable climbs and descents, wash crossings, obstacles, hazards, major turns and junctions—along the ride. All distances were measured to the nearest tenth of a mile with a carefully calibrated cyclometer. As a result, you will find a cyclometer very useful for following the descriptions. Terrain, riding technique, and even tire pressure can affect odometer readings, so treat all mileages as estimates. Trails were precisely mapped using the USGS 7.5-minute topographic maps as a reference. A GPS (Global Positioning System) receiver was used to supplement more traditional methods of land navigation where landmarks were obscure.

An options section at the end of the ride log lists possible variations on the ride, if any.

Finally, one last reminder: the real world is changing all the time. The information presented here is as accurate and up-to-date as possible, but there are no guarantees out in the backcountry. You, alone, are responsible for your safety and for the choices you make on the trail.

If you do find an error or omission in this book or a new and noteworthy change in a ride, I'd like to hear from you. Please write to Bruce Grubbs, c/o Falcon Publishing, P.O. Box 1718, Helena, Montana 59624.

The Name Game

Mountain bikers often assign their own descriptive nicknames to trails.

These nicknames may help to distinguish or describe certain parts of the overall ride, but only for the group of people who know the nickname. All too often the nicknames are meaningless—or misleading—to cyclists who haven't spun their pedals on the weekly group ride.

For the sake of clarity, I stuck to the official (or at least most widely accepted) names for the trails and roads described in this book. If you know them by some other name, or if you come up with nicknames that peg the personalities of these rides, then by all means share them with your riding buddies.

Maricopa Mountains

Margies Cove

Location: About 40 miles southwest of Goodyear.

Distance: 10.4 miles out and back.

Time: 2 hours.

Tread: Doubletrack.

Aerobic level: Easy.

Technical difficulty: 2.

Hazards: Loose sand and a few ruts.

Highlights: Very scenic and easy, this is a great ride for beginners and families. It takes you through an unspoiled example of Sonoran desert in the North Maricopa Mountains and ends in a wild basin that is surrounded by mountains.

Land status: State, Bureau of Land Management.

Maps: USGS Cotton Center NW, Margies Peak, Cotton Center SE.

Access: From Phoenix, drive west on Interstate 10 to Exit 112, then turn left (south) on Arizona Highway 85. Continue about 20 miles, then turn left (east) onto an obscure, unmarked dirt road at an old corral, and park near the highway.

Margies Cove

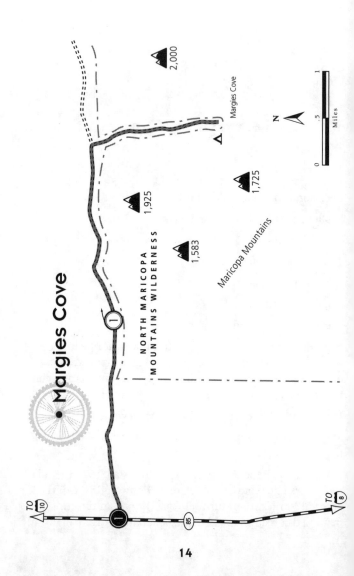

2,000

NORTH MARICOPA
MOUNTAINS WILDERNESS

1,925

1,583

1,725

Margies Cove

Maricopa Mountains

N

0   .5   1
Miles

TO 10

85

TO 8

14

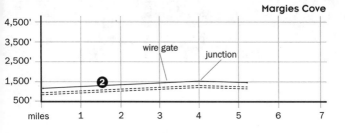

Margies Cove

The ride

0.0 Ride east on the doubletrack toward the Maricopa Mountains. After about a mile the road skirts the base of the mountains as you enter a canyon.

3.3 Go through a wire gate.

4.0 Turn right (south) on an unmarked road. The North Maricopa Mountains Wilderness boundary is on both sides of the road; please stay on it. As you cruise south, the mountains open up into a beautiful desert basin.

5.2 Reach Margies Cove Trailhead and campground. The trails beyond this point are in the wilderness, which is closed to bikes. Turn around and head back the way you came.

10.4 Back at the trailhead.

White Tank Mountain Regional Park

Technical Loop

Location: Northwest of Goodyear.

Distance: 5.9-mile loop.

Time: 1.5 hours.

Tread: Singletrack.

Aerobic level: Moderate.

Technical difficulty: 4.

Hazards: Deep sand and gravel at wash crossings; rocky sections.

Highlights: This ride is the longest loop available on the park's Sonoran Loop competitive track trail system, and it's a fine ride through classic desert. It combines a short technical section with a most enjoyable loop across the desert slopes below the mountains. If desired, you can bypass the technical section. These trails were designed for mountain-bike training and racing and are all one way. You can ride the trails at any speed you wish, but slower riders should give way to faster riders.

Land status: White Tank Mountain Regional Park.

• Technical Loop

WHITE TANK MOUNTAIN
REGIONAL PARK

Park
Headquarters

N

0   .5   1
Miles

TO
OLIVE AVENUE

Maps: USGS White Tank Mountains SE, Waddell; park trail map.

Access: From Phoenix, drive west on Interstate 10, then exit at Cotton Lane and turn right. Go north 7.4 miles, then turn left onto Olive Avenue. Continue 4 miles to the park entrance station, then follow White Tank Mountain Drive another 3.6 miles to its end at the trailhead.

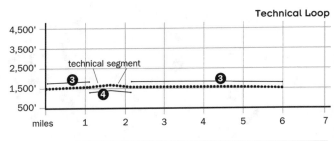

Technical Loop

The ride

0.0 Cross a wash and ride past a trail that merges from the right. You'll ride generally west toward the mountains, climbing gradually.

1.2 Hang a left onto the technical segment. Pedal up a slightly steeper, though still easy, climb.

1.7 The high point of the ride and the beginning of the most difficult stretch, as you wind around boulders and in and out of gullies right at the base of the mountains.

2.2 Rejoin the main loop by turning left.

2.6 Stay left at this junction and continue north.

3.3 The trail turns sharply right, toward the southeast, and zigzags across the desert, descending slightly.

4.7 A trail merges from the right just as you start down into a wash.

5.8 The trailhead is visible ahead—go left to get there.

(The right fork bypasses the trailhead. Take it if you want to repeat the loop.)

5.9 End of the ride at the trailhead.

Options: At 1.2 miles, go straight ahead to bypass the technical section. This makes the ride slightly shorter at 5.7 miles, and easier: now it's a Level-3 ride.

Sonoran Loop

Location: Northwest of Goodyear.

Distance: 3.9-mile loop.

Time: 1.5 hours.

Tread: Singletrack.

Aerobic level: Moderate.

Technical difficulty: 3.

Hazards: Deep sand and gravel at wash crossings; rocky sections.

Highlights: This ride is an easier and shorter variation on the Technical Loop, Ride 2. These trails were designed for mountain-bike training and racing and are all one way. You can ride the trails at any speed you wish, but slower riders should give way to faster riders.

Land status: White Tank Mountain Regional Park.

Maps: USGS White Tank Mountains SE, Waddell; park trail map.

• Sonoran Loop

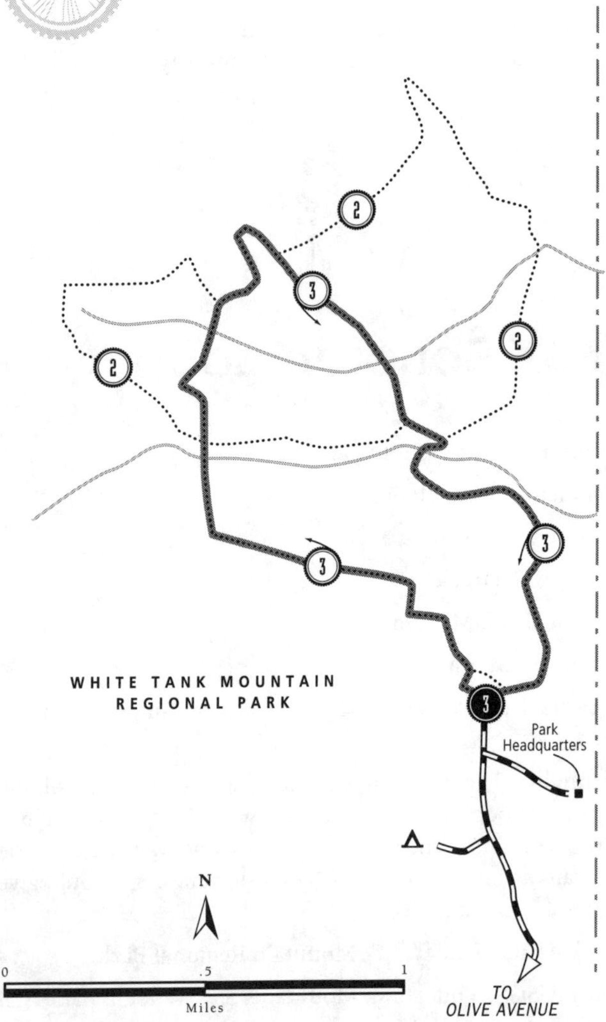

WHITE TANK MOUNTAIN
REGIONAL PARK

Park
Headquarters

N

0   .5   1
Miles

TO
OLIVE AVENUE

20

Access: From Phoenix, drive west on Interstate 10, then exit at Cotton Lane and turn right. Go north 7.4 miles, then turn left onto Olive Avenue. Continue 4 miles to the park entrance station, then follow White Tank Mountain Drive another 3.6 miles to its end at the trailhead.

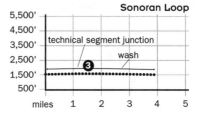

The ride

0.0 Cross a wash and continue past the trail that merges from the right. You'll be climbing very gradually, heading west toward the mountains.

1.2 Go straight at the technical segment junction.

2.0 Branch right onto a trail that runs southeast and slightly downhill.

2.6 A trail merges from the right.

2.7 The main loop merges from the left; turn sharply right to join it and cross a wash.

3.8 Go left to the trailhead, or go right if you wish to repeat the loop or a variation of it.

3.9 Trailhead.

Options: At the technical segment junction at 1.2 miles, hang a sharp right to make the smallest possible loop. It's 3.1 miles, aerobically easy, and technically a 3.

Estrella Mountain Regional Park

Rainbow Valley Loop

Location: Southwest of Goodyear.

Distance: 6.2-mile loop.

Time: 1.5 hours.

Tread: Singletrack.

Aerobic level: Moderate.

Technical difficulty: 3 with short sections of 4 and 4+.

Hazards: This is the desert, so there's deep, loose sand and gravel at wash crossings and some rocky sections. There are numerous unsigned trail junctions and unofficial trails; following the most heavily used trail will keep you on this loop. The park is in the process of re-evaluating its trail system, so the situation should improve in the future. Watch for hikers, horses, and other riders.

Highlights: This is a great loop through the northwestern end of the Sierra Estrella. It passes through the edge of Rainbow Valley and offers some short but challenging technical work.

Land status: Estrella Mountain Regional Park.

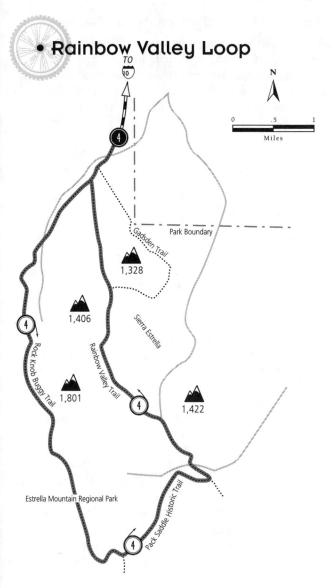

Rainbow Valley Loop

TO
10

N

0   .5   1
Miles

Park Boundary

Gadsden Trail

1,328

Sierra Estrella

1,406

Rock Knob Buggy Trail

Rainbow Valley Trail

1,801

1,422

Estrella Mountain Regional Park

Pack Saddle Historic Trail

Maps: USGS Perryville, Tolleson, Avondale SW, Avondale SE.

Access: From Phoenix, go west on Interstate 10 to Exit 126, then turn left (south) on Estrella Parkway. Drive 5.2 miles, then turn left onto Vineyard Drive. After 0.6 miles, turn right into the park entrance. Continue 2.1 miles to the end of the road at the rodeo arena. The trailhead is on the left side of the parking area.

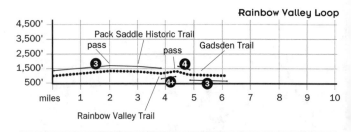

Rainbow Valley Loop

The ride

0.0   Start on the Rock Knob Buggy Trail, an old road that's now a broad singletrack.

0.1   Cross a wash and pass the Rainbow Valley Trail turn-off, which is on the left. This will be our return. For now, pedal on up the smooth, fast old road as it climbs gradually southward up the mountain valley.

0.7   Follow the old road as it veers right to cross a wash. The climb steepens a bit and the tread is rocky in places.

2.1   Cross a pass overlooking Rainbow Valley, the immense desert valley west of the Sierra Estrella, and start down toward the southeast. The tread becomes smooth and fast, a suitable reward for having jounced over the rocks leading to the pass.

2.9   Hang a left, staying on the main trail, onto Pack Saddle Historic Trail. Now you'll be riding almost east.

24

3.8   Cross a wash, then swing sharply left onto Rainbow Valley Trail, still the most heavily used trail. The tread becomes narrow singletrack and heads generally north, climbing toward a pass.

4.4   A final steep, but short,climb takes you to a pass with a panoramic view of the surrounding rugged mountains and hills. An equally short, steep descent leads to a trail junction; stay left.

4.8   A minor trail branches left; lean to the right to stay on the main trail.

5.1   Gadsden Trail forks right; go left and cross a wash. The arena and trailhead is visible ahead. This section is fast, smooth tread.

6.1   Rejoin Rock Knob Buggy Trail at the wash; hang a right to return to the trailhead.

6.2   End of the ride at the arena.

Option: Take the Gadsden Trail at mile 5.1 to add another challenging section.

5.1   Turn right on Gadsden Trail, which is unmarked and just before a wash crossing. You'll be climbing gradually at first, then you'll cross a pass and descend to the east.

5.5   Pedal left at a T intersection and start to climb northwest.

5.8   A steep, loose, rocky climb leads to a fence corner where you'll start an equally steep, loose, rocky descent. At least it's short.

6.3   Hang a right on Rainbow Valley Trail, drop into a wash, and turn right again on Rock Knob Buggy Trail.

6.4   End of the ride at the arena and trailhead.

South Mountain Park

Pima Loop

Location: South Phoenix.

Distance: 3.1-mile loop.

Time: 0.5 hour.

Tread: Singletrack.

Aerobic level: Moderate.

Technical difficulty: 4.

Hazards: Steep, rocky areas; sections of loose gravel. These are heavily used trails—watch for hikers, horses, and other riders.

Highlights: This ride combines Loop One and Loop Two Trails into a short, but challenging, ride north of Pima Canyon Trailhead. The area is laced with many trails that can be confusing, but it's difficult to get lost.

Land status: Phoenix South Mountain Park.

Maps: USGS Guadalupe.

Access: From Interstate 10, exit at Elliot Road, then go west 0.5 mile to 48th Street. Turn right (north), and go 1 mile to Guadalupe Road. One block north of Guadalupe, turn left and drive to the Pima Canyon Trailhead at the end of the road.

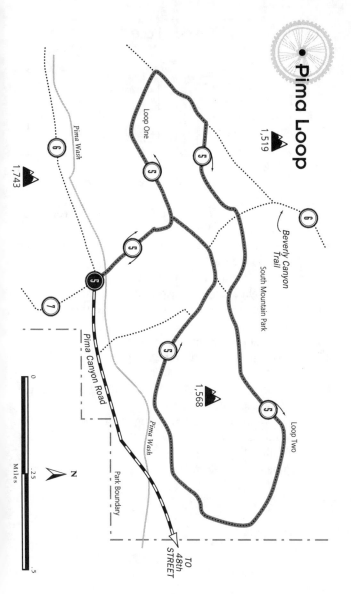

Pima Loop

1,519

1,743

1,568

Loop One

Loop Two

Pima Wash

Pima Wash

Pima Canyon Road

Park Boundary

Beverly Canyon Trail

South Mountain Park

N

TO 48th STREET

Miles

0   .25   .5

27

The ride

0.0 Start at the north ramada, ride across Pima Wash Trail, then climb over a steep ridge.

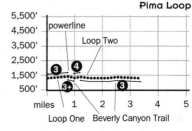

0.3 Hang a left to start the loop section.

0.7 Go right to stay on Loop One Trail as it veers away from the powerline.

1.0 Cross Beverly Canyon Trail and ride over the steep ridge to the east.

1.2 Pedal left at a T intersection to join Loop Two.

1.4 Bear right at an unnamed trail junction.

1.6 Bear right again. The trail climbs a bit, then contours above the golf course.

2.1 Stay right yet again.

2.2 Stay right (the trail to the left goes to Pima Canyon Road).

2.4 Beverly Canyon Trail merges from right—continue straight ahead.

2.5 End of the loop section; hang a left to return to the trailhead.

2.8 Trailhead.

3.1 Pima Canyon Road and the end of the ride.

Javelina Loop

Location: South Phoenix.

Distance: 5.6-mile loop.

Time: 1.5 hours.

Tread: Singletrack.

Aerobic level: Moderate.

Technical difficulty: 3 with a short section of 4- (the Ridgeline option is 4+).

Hazards: The usual steep, rocky areas and sections of loose gravel. Watch for other trail users.

Highlights: This is a very enjoyable loop with only a few difficult sections.

Land status: Phoenix South Mountain Park.

Maps: USGS Guadalupe, Lone Butte.

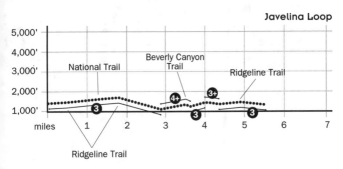

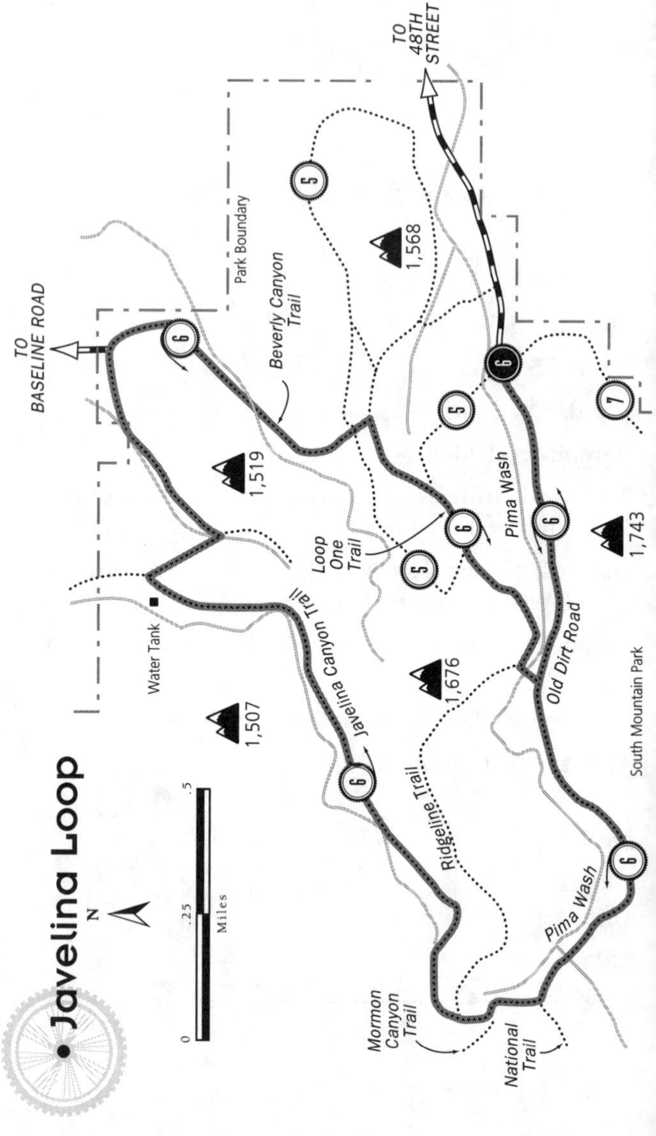

Javelina Loop

N

Miles
0   .25   .5

TO BASELINE ROAD

TO 48TH STREET

Park Boundary

Beverly Canyon Trail

1,568

1,519

Loop One Trail

Javelina Canyon Trail

Water Tank

1,507

Ridgeline Trail

1,676

Pima Wash

Old Dirt Road

1,743

South Mountain Park

Mormon Canyon Trail

National Trail

Pima Wash

30

Access: From Interstate 10, exit at Elliot Road, then go west 0.5 mile to 48th Street. Turn right (north), and go 1 mile to Guadalupe Road. One block north of Guadalupe, turn left and drive to the Pima Canyon Trailhead at the end of the road.

The ride

0.0	Start from the north ramada and go west on the old dirt road.
0.6	Ridgeline Trail comes in from the right; this will be our return.
1.3	The old dirt road ends; continue on the National Trail. Pass the Pima Wash turnoff, then hang a right onto Mormon Canyon Trail.
1.6	Go right onto Javelina Canyon Trail and climb a short, steep hill.
1.7	At the top of the ridge, which is also the high point of the ride, continue straight ahead (Ridgeline Trail goes right).
2.9	You'll ride around a large water-storage tank, then hang a right to follow the trail over a ridge.
3.4	At a T intersection, go left, downhill.
3.5	Ride across the parking area at the 46th Street Trailhead and start Beverly Canyon Trail.
4.0	Go right to stay under the powerline and climb a short, steep hill.
4.1	Now veer left away from the powerline.
4.2	Cross over a ridge and Loop One Trail.
4.3	At a T intersection, hang a right onto Loop One.
4.4	Go straight, remaining on Loop One (the trail to the left is a 0.3-mile shortcut back to the trailhead).
4.6	Go straight (Loop One goes right).
4.8	At Pima Wash Trail, hang a right.

4.9　Turn left onto Ridgeline Trail, and follow it across the wash and up to the old dirt road. Turn left and cruise down to the trailhead.

5.6　Trailhead and the end of the ride.

Option: At mile 1.7, turn right on Ridgeline Trail for a shorter, but very challenging, variation with lots of short, steep climbs.

2.6　Hang a right under the powerline.

2.7　Go right onto Pima Wash Trail, then immediately left out of the wash to rejoin the old dirt road. Hang a left and cruise down to the parking area.

3.4　Trailhead at the north ramada.

Desert Classic Trail

Location: South Phoenix.

Distance: 17.6 miles out and back.

Time: 4 hours.

Tread: Singletrack.

Aerobic level: Moderate.

Technical difficulty: 3.

Hazards: Loose sand and gravel in wash crossings; occasional rocky sections. Watch for hikers and other riders.

Highlights: This well-named trail is a delightful cruise along the foothills of South Mountain. The route lies in the narrow

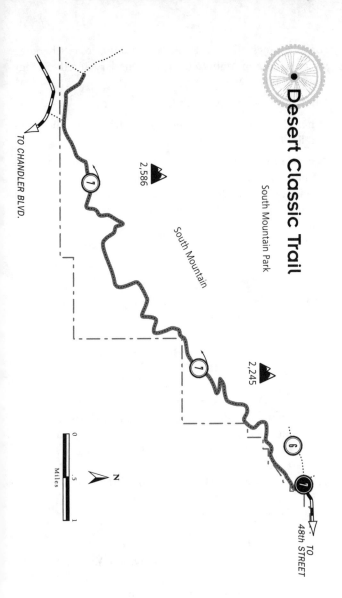

Desert Classic Trail

South Mountain Park

TO CHANDLER BLVD.

2,586

South Mountain

2,245

TO 48th STREET

N
Miles
0 .5 1

corridor of desert foothills between the suburbs of Chandler, which have crept right to the park boundary, and the craggy slopes of South Mountain.

Land status: Phoenix South Mountain Park.

Maps: USGS Guadalupe, Lone Butte; Phoenix South Mountain Park brochure.

Access: From Interstate 10, exit at Elliot Road, then go west 0.5 mile to 48th Street. Turn right (north), and go 1 mile to Guadalupe Road. One block north of Guadalupe, turn left and drive to the Pima Canyon Trailhead at the end of the road.

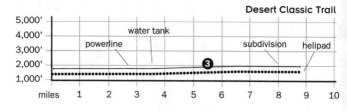

Desert Classic Trail

The ride

0.0   The Desert Classic Trail starts from the ramadas at the south side of the parking area and skirts the south slopes of the mountain. There are numerous minor side trails, but the main trail is well marked and easy to follow.

2.7   Follow a powerline for a short distance to the south.

3.7   Go around the north side of a water tank.

5.0   Pedal left at a junction.

5.1   Stay right at this junction.

6.6   Stay right again.

8.0   The trail runs next to a subdivision. You can leave the ride here and return to the trailhead by riding south to Chandler Boulevard, east to Ray Road, north and east to 48th Street, then north to Pima Canyon Road, a distance of 10 miles along streets with painted bike lanes.

8.8   Turn around at a concrete helipad. This is the start of the steep, rocky Telegraph Pass Trail, which climbs to the saddle north of you. The fun way to return is to reverse the ride, but you can also use the city streets as mentioned above.

17.6   Back at the trailhead.

Phoenix Mountains Preserve

Trail 100

Location: North Phoenix.

Distance: 21.6 miles out and back, or 10.8 miles one way with a shuttle.

Time: 4 hours.

Tread: Singletrack.

Aerobic level: Moderate.

Technical difficulty: 3.

Hazards: Loose gravel at wash crossings, a few steep sections, and a few rocky places. Watch for other riders, hikers, and equestrians.

Highlights: This great ride traverses the Phoenix Mountains Preserve from Shaw Butte at the west end to northeast of Squaw Peak at the east end. All the street crossings are via underpasses. The best way to do the ride is with a shuttle, but you could ride out and back for a real workout or return via the city streets.

Land status: Phoenix Mountains Preserve.

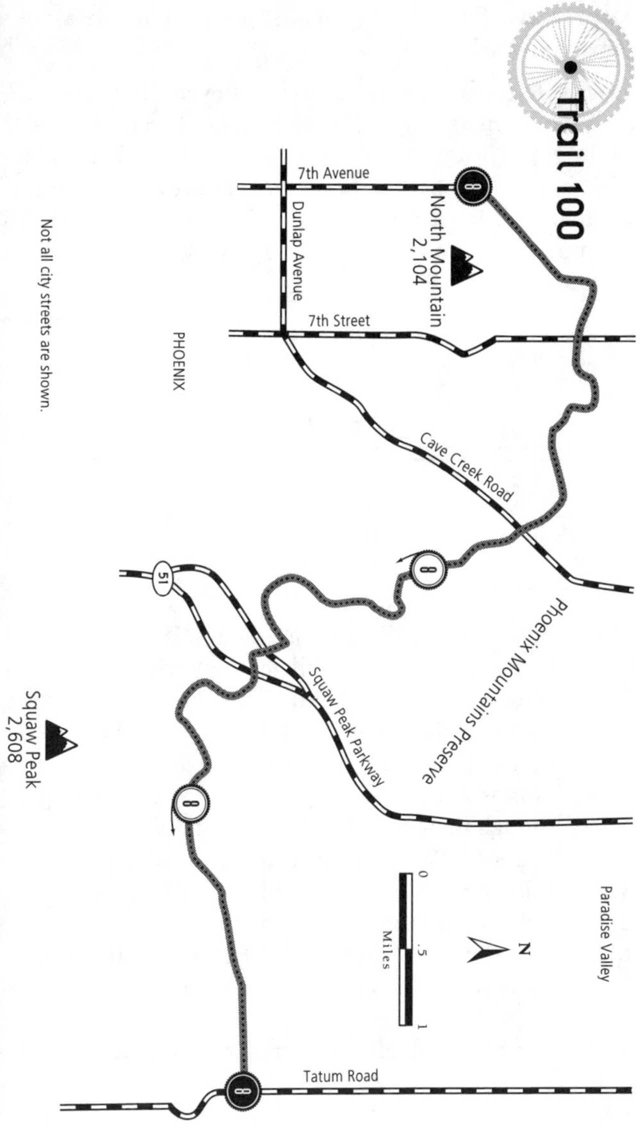

Trail 100

Not all city streets are shown.

PHOENIX

7th Avenue

Dunlap Avenue

7th Street

North Mountain
2,104

Cave Creek Road

Phoenix Mountains Preserve

51

Squaw Peak Parkway

Squaw Peak
2,608

Paradise Valley

N

0   .5   1
Miles

Tatum Road

37

Maps: USGS Sunnyslope, Paradise Valley; Phoenix Mountains Preserve brochure.

Access: To reach the end of the ride with your shuttle vehicle, drive north on Tatum Road to the trailhead on the west side of the street just north of Sunset Lane. Parking here is limited; you can also park along Tatum on the east side south of the trailhead. To reach the start of the ride, drive north on 7th Avenue to its end (north of Dunlap Road) at the Trail 100 Trailhead.

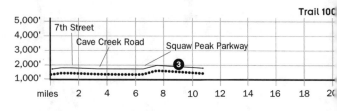

The ride

0.0   Trail 100 goes north from the trailhead toward the low saddle and is well marked with steel posts throughout its length. There are numerous side trails, some official, some not. Please stay on the marked, official trails, and respect all closed areas. The route climbs and descends gradually for the most part, though there are a few short, steep hills.

0.7   Cross over a saddle and start a gradual descent.

1.6   Ride under 7th Street (trailhead on the west side).

3.5   Cross under Cave Creek Road.

6.6   Cross under Squaw Peak Parkway (trailhead at Dreamy Draw Recreation Area on the east side of freeway).

7.8   Top of a gradual-to-moderate climb north of Squaw Peak.

9.9   Cross a gentle pass; start down toward the houses.

10.8 Tatum Road and the end of the ride. Either turn around and head back the way you came or pick up your shuttle vehicle.

21.6 Back at the trailhead.

Options: You could return via Tatum Road, Lincoln Boulevard, the Arizona Canal trail, and 7th Avenue. This option is 11.4 miles and takes about an hour. Use caution—there are no bike lanes on the city streets. The pleasant trail along the Arizona Canal has underpasses at the major streets.

McDowell Mountains

Dynamite Loop

Location: In Scottsdale at the intersection of Pima and Dynamite Roads.

Distance: 12.3-mile loop.

Time: 2 hours.

Tread: 3.4 miles singletrack; 8.9 miles doubletrack.

Aerobic level: Easy.

Technical difficulty: 3- on singletrack; 2+ on doubletrack.

Hazards: Occasional loose, gravelly areas, especially crossing washes. Watch for other riders, as well as ATVs.

Highlights: This is a fine section of Sonoran, granite boulder-studded desert with numerous singletrack and doubletrack trails. A double powerline runs north-northeast from the intersection of Pima and Dynamite Roads and forms the baseline for the area. A loop using trails west of the powerline outbound, with a return along the powerline doubletrack is described here, but there are many other possibilities on both sides. You can explore away from the powerline, then make your way back to it for a fast return to the trailhead. Urban sprawl is fast encroaching on this area, so enjoy it while it lasts.

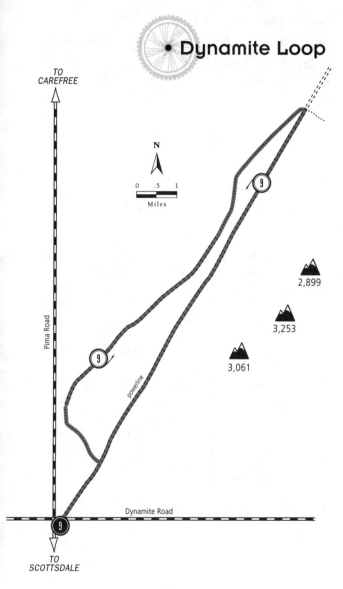

• Dynamite Loop

TO
CAREFREE

N

0   .5   1
Miles

Pima Road

9

9

powerline

2,899

3,253

3,061

Dynamite Road

9

TO
SCOTTSDALE

41

Land status: State.

Maps: USGS Cave Creek, Currys Corner, Wildcat Hill.

Access: From Scottsdale, go north on Pima Road to Dynamite Road. Park on the southeast corner under the double powerline.

The ride

0.0 Follow the double powerline across busy Dynamite Road. Use caution! (There is also a single powerline, which runs more northeasterly than the double powerline.)

0.8 Go left on a singletrack and cross under the west powerline. You'll be riding up and over small, fun hills; watch for other riders on the blind curves.

1.5 Cross a wash and ride north on the singletrack.

1.7 Join a doubletrack at a clearing and continue generally north. The double powerline will always be in sight to the east.

2.5 A road goes right; pedal straight ahead.

3.9 Ride through an old gate.

4.1 Go left on singletrack. This is an especially fun section; you'll swoop through dips and fast corners.

6.6 The singletrack crosses under the double powerline; hang a right onto the doubletrack and follow the powerlines south-southwest.

8.6 Ride through an old gate.

9.4 Go through another gate.

11.0 Yet another gate.

12.3 End of the ride at Pima and Dynamite Roads.

Sport Loop

Location: About 22 miles east of Scottsdale in McDowell Mountain Regional Park.

Distance: 3.0-mile loop.

Time: 0.5 hour.

Tread: Singletrack.

Aerobic level: Moderate.

Technical difficulty: 3+.

Hazards: Loose gravel in wash crossings; sudden sharp dips in ravines.

Highlights: This short, but fun, loop is part of the competitive track system at the park. It was designed specifically for skilled riders, high speeds, and racing, and has sharp turns and abrupt transitions as it passes through roller-coaster terrain. Though you can ride at any speed, slower riders should give way to faster riders. The loop is one way. You should ride the track at a reasonable speed the first time to become familiar with it.

Land status: McDowell Mountain Regional Park

Maps: USGS Fort McDowell; park map.

Access: From Scottsdale on Shea Boulevard, go east to Fountain Hills Boulevard, then turn left. After you drive through the subdivision, the road becomes McDowell Mountain Road; turn left at the sign into McDowell Mountain Regional

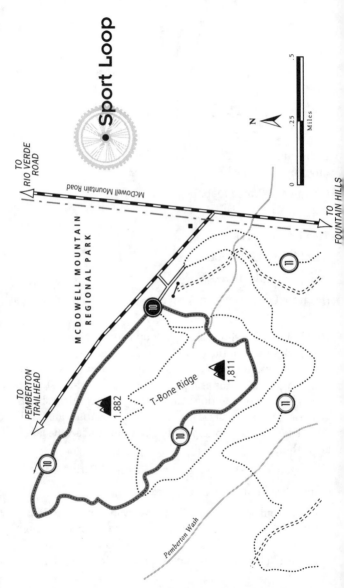

Sport Loop

TO RIO VERDE ROAD

McDowell Mountain Road

MCDOWELL MOUNTAIN REGIONAL PARK

TO PEMBERTON TRAILHEAD

TO FOUNTAIN HILLS

T-Bone Ridge

1,882

1,811

Pemberton Wash

N

0   .25   .5
Miles

Park. You can reach this same turnoff from Scottsdale Road at Dynamite Road by proceeding east on Dynamite, which becomes Rio Verde Road. Go 15 miles, then turn right (south) onto Forest Road at a T intersection. After 2.1 miles turn right onto McDowell Mountain Road, then go another 4.5 miles and turn right into the park. The trailhead is just past the entrance station on the left, at the competitive track parking area. There is an entrance fee for the park.

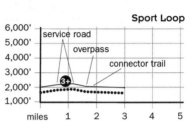

The ride

0.0 Start at the west end of the parking area. At first, you'll be working your way northwest along the base of the north side of T-Bone Ridge.

0.6 Cross a wash and a service road.

1.1 The trail turns south and crosses the service road again.

1.6 Pedal across the Expert Loop on an overpass (no trail junction).

1.7 At the connector trail to the Expert Loop, go left.

1.8 Another connector trail; ride straight ahead.

3.0 Ride into the parking area about midway down its length.

Long Loop

Location: About 22 miles east of Scottsdale in McDowell Mountain Regional Park.

Distance: 8.1-mile loop.

Time: 1.5 hours.

Tread: Singletrack.

Aerobic level: Moderate.

Technical difficulty: 3+.

Hazards: Loose gravel in wash crossings; sudden sharp dips in ravines.

Highlights: This is the longest of the three loops that make up the competitive track system at the park. It was designed specifically for skilled riders, high speeds, and racing, and has sharp turns and abrupt transitions as it passes through roller-coaster terrain. Though you can ride at any speed, slower riders should give way to faster riders. The loop is one way. You should ride the track at a reasonable speed the first time to become familiar with it.

Land status: McDowell Mountain Regional Park

Maps: USGS Fort McDowell; park map.

Access: From Shea Boulevard, go east to Fountain Hills Boulevard, then turn left. After you drive through the subdivision, the road becomes McDowell Mountain Road; turn left at the sign into McDowell Mountain Regional Park. You can reach this same turnoff from Scottsdale Road at Dynamite

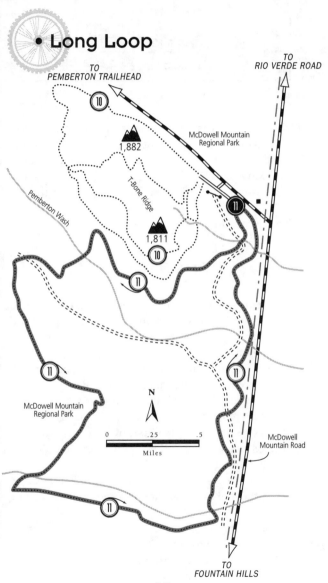

Long Loop

TO
PEMBERTON TRAILHEAD

TO
RIO VERDE ROAD

(10)

McDowell Mountain
Regional Park

▲
1,882

T-Bone Ridge

Pemberton Wash

▲
1,811

(10)

(11)

(11)

(11)

(11)

McDowell Mountain
Regional Park

N

0   .25   .5
Miles

McDowell
Mountain Road

(11)

TO
FOUNTAIN HILLS

47

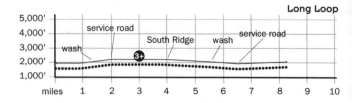

Road by proceeding east on Dynamite, which becomes Rio Verde Road. Go 15 miles, then turn right (south) onto Forest Road at a T intersection. After 2.1 miles turn right onto McDowell Mountain Road, then go another 4.5 miles and turn right into the park. The trailhead is just past the entrance station on the left, at the competitive track parking area. There is an entrance fee for the park.

The ride

0.0 The entrance to this one-way loop is at the east end of the parking area. Drop down a short, steep hill and cross a wash and service road. Now the trail turns to the southwest.

0.7 A one-way trail merges from the right, and the trail turns northwest as it swings around T-Bone Ridge, the prominent hill west of the parking area.

1.6 Cross Pemberton Wash.

2.0 Cross a service road. The trail swings south, and there's a great view of the Superstition Mountains to the southeast.

4.1 Ride across another wash and up onto South Ridge. Here the trail turns east and descends gradually along the ridge crest.

5.6 Drop off the ridge to the north and cross the wash.

6.5 Cross a service road.

8.1 The trail ends at the east end of the parking area.

Pemberton Trail

Location: About 22 miles east of Scottsdale in McDowell Mountain Regional Park.

Distance: 15.6-mile loop.

Time: 3 hours.

Tread: Singletrack.

Aerobic level: Moderate.

Technical difficulty: 3.

Hazards: A few short, rocky sections on otherwise smooth tread. There are numerous sharp transitions at wash crossings, especially in the roller-coaster section. Watch for riders coming the other direction on this popular trail. And of course, keep an eye out for hikers and horses.

Highlights: This is a most enjoyable, classic singletrack loop across the eastern slope of the McDowell Mountains. It's a fast, nontechnical loop with just enough variety for its length. The ride is best done clockwise, though it's certainly rideable either direction. The trail is well marked.

Land status: McDowell Mountain Regional Park.

Maps: USGS Fort McDowell, McDowell Peak; park map.

Access: From Shea Boulevard, go east to Fountain Hills Boulevard, then turn left. After you drive through the subdivision, the road becomes McDowell Mountain Road; turn left at the sign into McDowell Mountain Regional Park. You can

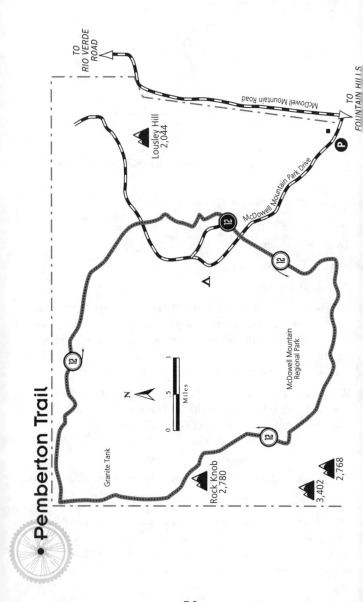

Pemberton Trail

TO
RIO VERDE
ROAD

Lousley Hill
2,044

McDowell Mountain Road

TO
FOUNTAIN HILLS

P

McDowell Mountain Park Drive

12

12

McDowell Mountain
Regional Park

N

1
.5
0

Miles

Granite Tank

Rock Knob
2,780

3,402

2,768

12

12

12

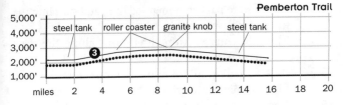

reach this same turnoff from Scottsdale Road at Dynamite Road by proceeding east on Dynamite, which becomes Rio Verde Road. Go 15 miles, then turn right (south) onto Forest Road at a T intersection. After 2.1 miles turn right onto McDowell Mountain Road, then go another 4.5 miles and turn right into the park. The trailhead is past the campground on the right, at the group area. There is an entrance fee for the park.

The ride

0.0 Start from the south side of the parking area and ride south on smooth singletrack that's nearly level. You'll soon cross the paved park road.

0.6 Junction with the Granite Trail, which is closed to bikes. Ride straight ahead.

1.6 Cruise past a steel water tank, then curve southeast below some bluffs.

1.9 The trail swings south again, then starts a gradual climb to the west.

2.3 Crank up a steeper, somewhat rocky, section.

2.5 Now ride a gradually ascending ridge toward the mountains.

4.3 The trail turns more to the northwest as it nears the steep slopes of the mountains and climbs a little more.

4.9	Stay right to pass an unmarked trail, and start into the fun roller-coaster section.
6.3	The following section runs north along the west boundary of the park.
8.6	Pass a small granite knob and Granite Tank at the highest point of the ride.
9.2	Hang a sharp right as the trail turns east. This is a fast cruise down a long, gradual descent. Keep your speed under control and be alert for other riders as well as hikers and horses.
12.6	Pass another steel water tank.
14.1	Cross the paved park road.
15.6	Trailhead and the end of the ride.

Cave Creek
Recreation Area

New River Loop

Location: About 8 miles east of Cave Creek.

Distance: 6.4-mile loop.

Time: 1.5 hours.

Tread: 2.4 miles singletrack; 1.2 miles dirt road; 0.9 mile maintained dirt road; 1.9 miles paved.

Aerobic level: Easy.

Technical difficulty: 3+ on singletrack, 2 on dirt roads, and 1 on pavement.

Hazards: Some rocky sections and a few sandy areas.

Highlights: This is the least rocky of the trails in the park. It traverses a beautiful section of classic Sonoran desert, then returns via an easy roll down a dirt road and the paved park entrance road.

Land status: Maricopa County Park.

Maps: USGS New River SE, Cave Creek.

Access: From Interstate 17 north of Phoenix, take Carefree Highway east about 6 miles to 32nd Street, turn left, and go 1.5 miles north to the park. Continue to the picnic area and

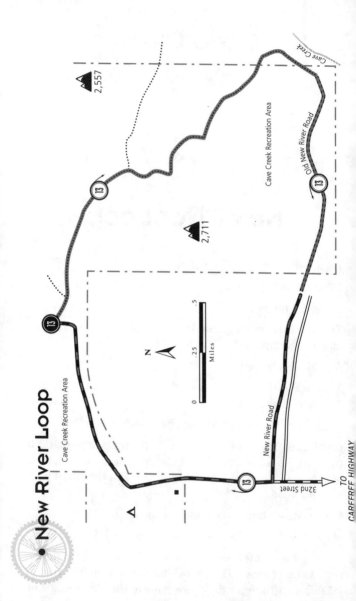

New River Loop

2,557

2,711

Cave Creek

Cave Creek Recreation Area

Old New River Road

Cave Creek Recreation Area

N

Miles
0   .25   .5

New River Road

32nd Street

TO
CAREFREE HIGHWAY

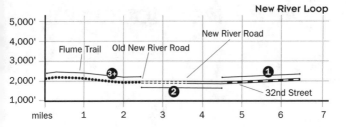

New River Loop

trailhead at the end of the road. Or, from Cave Creek Road south of Cave Creek, go 3 miles west on Carefree Highway to reach 32nd Street and turn right. There is an entrance fee for cars.

The ride

0.0   Start on the Slate Trail and ride generally east through gently rolling desert. The trail, which is rocky in places, climbs gradually.

0.2   Ride straight ahead to stay on the Slate Trail.

0.4   Cross a broad pass.

0.9   Go right at the junction with the Flume Trail (Slate Trail goes left). You'll ride down the wash and occasionally climb out via steep, rocky sections.

2.1   Emerge into the flood plain of Cave Creek and turn right just before a gate to stay on the Flume Trail as it runs southwest along the base of the hills.

2.4   Join the old New River Road, which is no longer maintained, and pedal east on its broad surface.

3.4   Go through a gate at the park boundary.

3.6   New River Road becomes maintained.

4.5   Turn right (north) on 32nd Street, which is paved with a bike lane, and ride back to Cave Creek Park.

6.4   Trailhead at the park picnic area and end of the ride.

New River Mountains

New River West

Location: About 22 miles north of Carefree.

Distance: 12.8 miles out and back.

Time: 4 hours.

Tread: Doubletrack.

Aerobic level: Strenuous.

Technical difficulty: 3-.

Hazards: Deep ruts, loose gravel, and several rocky stretches.

Highlights: This ride wanders west along New River, an intermittent stream flowing in a scenic canyon nestled between the New River Mountains and New River Mesa.

Land status: Tonto National Forest.

Maps: USGS Cooks Mesa, New River Mesa, Daisy Mountain; Tonto National Forest.

Access: From Carefree, drive about 17 miles north on Cave Creek Road, (which becomes Forest Road 24), then turn left onto FR 41. Continue 5.7 miles to the junction with FR 37 at New River, and park. Both FR 24 and FR 41 are dirt roads that are occasionally maintained. Except during wet weather, they are passable to most vehicles.

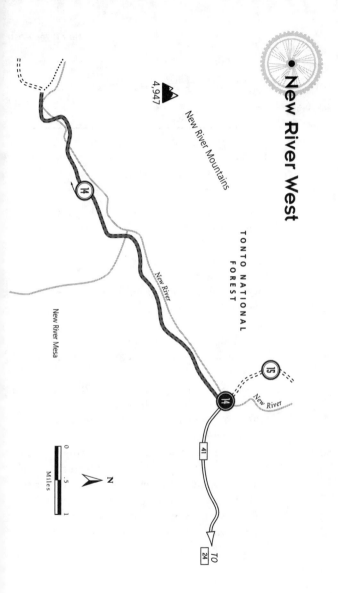

New River West

4,947

New River Mountains

TONTO NATIONAL FOREST

New River

New River Mesa

14

15

14

New River

41

TO 24

N

0 .5 1
Miles

57

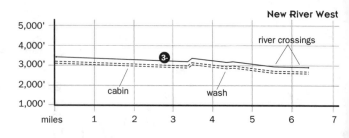

New River West

The ride

0.0	Ride west on FR 41 across a wash and up a short hill.
0.9	The road levels and smoothes out as it crosses the riverside flats.
1.9	Pedal past an old corral and cabin.
2.4	Go through a wire gate.
3.3	Start a rocky climb away from the river.
3.5	Cross a hillside and start down.
4.4	Rattle (or walk) across a very rocky wash crossing, then crank up a short, steep climb.
4.6	Pedal through a cholla-cactus-covered pass, then start a rocky descent.
4.7	You'll have smoother going for a while as the road stays on the flats close to the river.
5.5	Roll down a short, steep descent to cross the river at a very rocky crossing.
6.2	Cross the river at a another rocky crossing.
6.4	Turn around at the point where the road swings around a rock bluff then crosses a wash. After this point, the road climbs steeply to cross a shoulder of New River Mesa to avoid a narrow gorge along the river. It's rewarding to explore the gorge on foot.
12.8	Back at the trailhead.

New River Headwaters

Location: About 22 miles north of Carefree.

Distance: 6.8 miles out and back.

Time: 2 hours.

Tread: Doubletrack.

Aerobic level: Moderate.

Technical difficulty: 2+.

Hazards: Loose gravel, occasional deep ruts, and a few rocky sections.

Highlights: This ride follows the upper New River to a point near its headwaters. The road winds through granite boulder country, and the seasonal flow of the stream adds to the area's charm.

Land status: Tonto National Forest.

Maps: USGS Cooks Mesa; Tonto National Forest.

Access: From Carefree, drive about 17 miles north on Cave Creek Road, (which becomes Forest Road 24), then turn left onto FR 41. Continue 5.7 miles to the junction with FR 37 at New River, and park. Both FR 24 and FR 41 are dirt roads that are occasionally maintained.

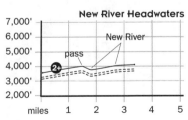

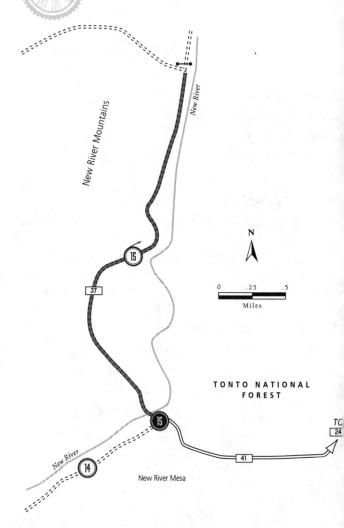

New River Headwaters

New River Mountains

New River

15

37

N

0   .25   .5
Miles

TONTO NATIONAL
FOREST

15

14

New River

41

TC
24

New River Mesa

Except during wet weather, they are passable to most vehicles.

The ride

0.0   Go right at the junction to start on FR 37, which immediately descends to cross New River. The river is actually an intermittent stream with flow that varies greatly with the season. It's easy to cross, except during or after heavy rain. The road now climbs away from the river to the west, winding through piles of granite boulders.

1.4   Cross a pass and start descending.

1.9   Pedal along the river's bank for a short distance, then start climbing again.

2.7   You've reached the top of the second climb—now the road parallels the river, which is a short distance to the east.

3.2   Pedal along a flat section next to the river.

3.4   Turn around at a locked gate marking the boundary of private property.

6.8   Back at the trailhead.

New River Mesa

Location: About 20 miles north of Carefree.

Distance: 4.2 miles out and back.

Time: 1 hour.

Tread: Doubletrack.

Aerobic level: Easy.

Technical difficulty: 2+.

Hazards: A few rocky sections.

Highlights: This easy ride follows a scenic ridge to the base of New River Mesa. You won't want to drive the long approach just for this ride, but if you're in the area, do it. Less-experienced members of groups may want to do this ride while the rock eaters are out bashing the tough stuff.

Land status: Tonto National Forest.

Maps: USGS Cooks Mesa, New River Mesa; Tonto National Forest.

Access: From Carefree, drive about 17 miles north on Cave Creek Road, (which becomes Forest Road 24), then turn left onto FR 41. Continue 2.8 miles to the junction with FR 17 on the left and park.

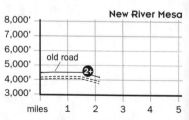

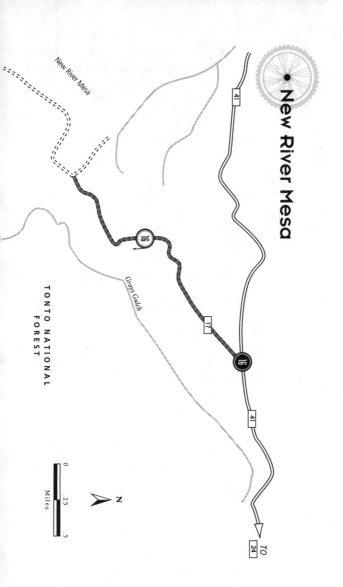

New River Mesa

TONTO NATIONAL FOREST

New River Mesa

Grays Gulch

N

Miles
0   .25   .5

TO 24

Both FR 24 and FR 41 are dirt roads that are occasionally maintained. Except during wet weather, they are passable to most vehicles.

The ride

0.0	Cruise down mostly smooth doubletrack through a valley.
0.3	Pedal across a saddle and start a short climb.
0.5	An old road merges from the right.
1.5	Bear right, then cruise down a hill with one short, steep, rocky section.
2.1	Roll into the broad saddle below New River Mesa, the flat-topped hill directly ahead. This is the turnaround point.
4.2	Back at the trailhead.

Options: If you're willing to put up with steep and rocky jeep tracks, you can ride (or walk) up the old road to the top of New River Mesa and then explore the old tracks made by ranchers putting in stock tanks.

Humboldt Mountain

Location: About 14 miles north of Carefree.

Distance: 7.8 miles out and back.

Time: 2 hours.

Tread: Paved.

Aerobic level: Strenuous.

Technical difficulty: 2-.

Hazards: Potholes in the beat-up pavement. Watch for on-coming traffic on the blind curves, especially during the descent.

Highlights: Super views of the mountains north and east of Phoenix.

Land status: Tonto National Forest.

Maps: USGS Humboldt Mountain; Tonto National Forest.

Access: From Carefree, drive about 14 miles north on Cave Creek Road, (which becomes Forest Road 24) to the junction with FR 562 and park.

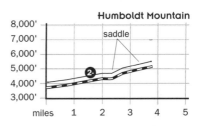

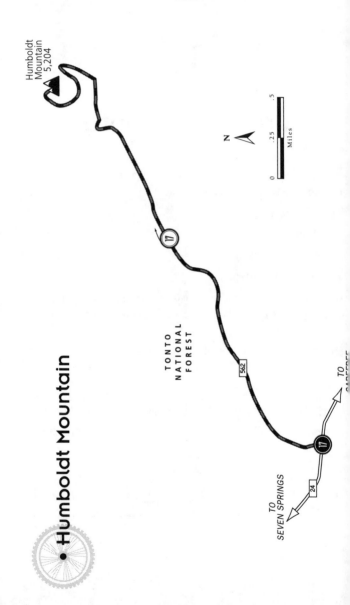

Humboldt Mountain

Humboldt
Mountain
5,204

TONTO
NATIONAL
FOREST

17

562

17

24

TO
SEVEN SPRINGS

TO
CAREFREE

N

0   .25   .5
Miles

The ride

0.0 Start off with a gradual climb along this narrow, rough, paved road. Your destination is clearly visible ahead; the summit is capped with a giant white "golf ball," which is an air traffic control radar site.

0.8 The climb steepens a bit.

2.0 Roll down a short downhill stretch.

2.2 The relentless (but not too long) climb starts again.

2.7 Pass through a broad saddle.

3.4 The road curves left through another saddle.

3.9 Reach the summit near the base of the fire lookout tower. You can walk or ride around the outside of the radar station fence to check out the stupendous views. The northern Mazatzal Mountains and the Verde River lie to the east; to the north you can see the distant Mogollon Rim; to the west the rugged skyline of the New River Mountains dominates; and to the south you get glimpses of the mountains around Phoenix. After checking out the view, turn around and enjoy the ride down.

7.8 Back at the trailhead.

Devils Hole

Location: About 14 miles east of Carefree.

Distance: 12.2 miles out and back.

Time: 3 hours.

Tread: Doubletrack.

Aerobic level: Strenuous.

Technical difficulty: 2+.

Hazards: Watch for deep, loose gravel on the downhill sections. Also be alert for oncoming vehicles on the blind curves.

Highlights: This is a straightforward ride though classic Sonoran desert that ends on the banks of the Verde River.

Land status: Tonto National Forest.

Maps: USGS Bartlett Dam, Horseshoe Dam; Tonto National Forest.

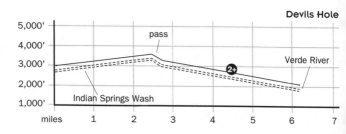

• Devils Hole

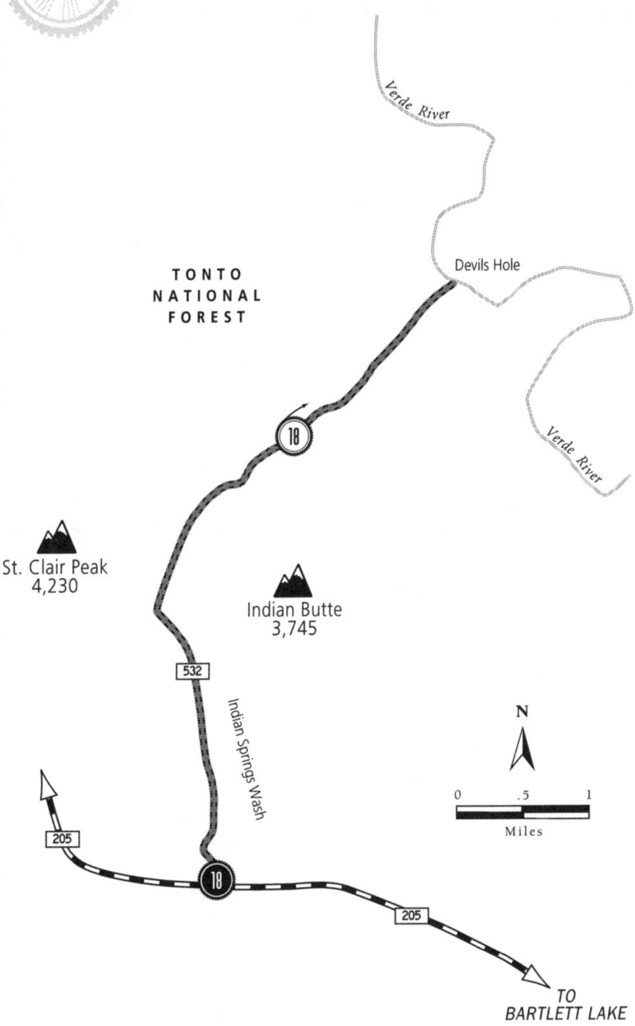

Verde River

Devils Hole

TONTO
NATIONAL
FOREST

Verde River

18

St. Clair Peak
4,230

Indian Butte
3,745

532

Indian Springs Wash

N

0   .5   1
Miles

205

18

205

TO
BARTLETT LAKE

69

Access: From Carefree, drive about 5 miles north on Cave Creek Road, then turn right onto Bartlett Lake Road (Forest Road 205). Follow this paved road 9.3 miles, then turn left onto Indian Springs Wash Road (FR 532) and park.

The ride

0.0	Pedal up a gradual climb as the doubletrack winds up along Indian Springs Wash.
1.4	Stay left on the main road. You're headed north toward a pass.
2.0	Climb up a steeper section onto a ridge.
2.4	Cross the pass, turn right, and start down the road that descends into the canyon to the north.
2.7	The descent moderates as the road drops into the wash.
4.2	Check out the view of the Mazatzal Mountains as the canyon walls start to open up.
6.1	The turnaround point is on the banks of the Verde River, one of the state's last free-flowing rivers.
12.2	Back at the trailhead.

Sheep Bridge

Location: About 22 miles northeast of Carefree.

Distance: 27 miles out and back.

Time: 4 hours.

Tread: Doubletrack.

Aerobic level: Moderate.

Technical difficulty: 2+.

Hazards: Some rocky stretches.

Highlights: This is a long cruise through the foothills of the Mazatzal Mountains to a historic suspension bridge on the Verde River.

Land status: Tonto National Forest.

Maps: USGS Horseshoe Dam, Chalk Mountain; Tonto National Forest.

Access: From Carefree, go about 5 miles north on Cave Creek Road, then turn right on Bartlett Lake Road (Forest Road 19). Continue 6.3 miles, then turn left on Horseshoe

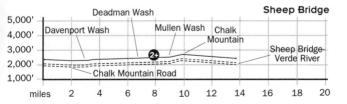

• Sheep Bridge

N

0   .5   1
Miles

269

Sheep Bridge

Verde River

TONTO NATIONAL FOREST

Ister Flat

Chalk Mountain
2,783

Mullen Wash

479

Deadman Wash

MAZATZAL WILDERNESS

Horseshoe Reservoir

19

TONTO NATIONAL FOREST

19

Davenport Wash

Verde River

205

TO CAREFREE

Dam Road (FR 205), which is maintained, but washboarded, dirt. A parking fee is required; you can pay and get your permit at the fee station 0.25 mile from the junction. Go 10.3 miles, then turn right on the Horseshoe Dam Viewpoint road. In another 0.5 mile, the road ends at a parking area below the dam.

The ride

0.0   Start by crossing the spillway structure via a walkway set under the spillway lip. This can be a dramatic crossing when the spillway is running! Then ride the dirt road south.

2.1   Go left onto Chalk Mountain Road, FR 479.

2.4   At a T intersection, ride left again to remain on Chalk Mountain Road.

3.1   Lean left at the Davenport Road turnoff, remaining on Chalk Mountain Road.

3.5   Start a steep, but short, climb out of Davenport Wash. You'll ride across several washes in the next few miles.

5.9   Rattle across a cattleguard at a corral.

6.7   Cross Deadman Wash, a major drainage from the mountains to the east.

9.2   Cross Mullen Wash, then climb toward the east side of Chalk Mountain.

9.8   Pedal over the high point of the ride, and start a descent toward Ister Flat.

13.5   Sheep Bridge and the turnaround point. The original bridge was built to get sheep over the Verde River as they were being moved from their winter range in the desert to summer ranges in the mountains, a practice that is still followed. A few years ago, the USDA Forest Service removed the dangerously deteriorated structure and built a new bridge. A road down Tangle

Creek on the west side of the river is the usual vehicle access, though the road you've just ridden can be reached via a river ford at Sheep Bridge and also downstream of Horseshoe Dam. At low water, both fords require a high-clearance vehicle, and during high water, they are impassable.

27.0 Back at the trailhead.

Usery Mountain Recreation Area

Blevins Loop

Location: Northeast Mesa.

Distance: 2.9-mile loop.

Time: 0.5 hour.

Tread: Singletrack.

Aerobic level: Easy.

Technical difficulty: 3.

Hazards: Loose gravel in washes. This is a heavily used trail; watch for horses, hikers, and other riders.

Highlights: This is an easy cruise on fun singletrack through classic desert. This short loop is especially good for families with very young riders. Numerous trails in this section of the park make possible several different loops—avoid the trails that follow washes because of deep sand. This ride and Moon Rock Loop are but two of the possibilities.

Land status: Usery Mountain Recreation Area, Tonto National Forest.

Maps: USGS Apache Junction.

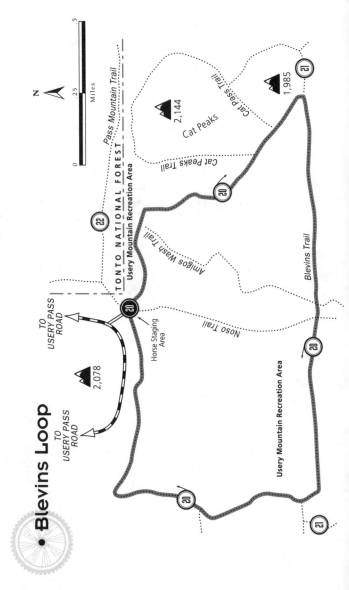

Blevins Loop

N

0   .25   .5
Miles

TO
USERY PASS ROAD

TO
USERY PASS ROAD

2,078

TONTO NATIONAL FOREST

Pass Mountain Trail

Cat Peaks

2,144

1,985

Cat Pass Trail

Cat Peaks Trail

Usery Mountain Recreation Area

Amigos Wash Trail

Blevins Trail

Noso Trail

Horse Staging Area

Usery Mountain Recreation Area

Access: From Mesa, go north on Ellsworth Road, which becomes Usery Pass Road. Turn right at the park entrance and go to the horse staging area, which is the trailhead.

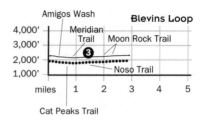

The ride

0.0 Ride smooth, easy singletrack, which is slightly downhill. Beginners may want to walk across a wash crossing near the start.

0.3 Continue straight past Amigos Wash Trail turnoff.

0.7 Cat Peaks Trail goes left; pedal straight ahead.

0.8 Cat Peaks Pass Trail goes left; continue straight ahead.

0.9 Now, Meridian Trail goes left; curve right on Blevins Trail.

1.1 Ride straight ahead at the junction with Nighthawk Wash Trail.

1.5 Pass Amigos Wash Trail and cross Noso Trail (this is a direct route back to the trailhead, if needed).

2.0 Cross Crismon Wash Trail, then bear right to stay on Blevins Trail at the junction with Moon Rock Trail. You'll be climbing very gradually.

2.3 Pass the upper Moon Rock Trail.

2.9 End of the ride at the horse staging area.

Moon Rock Loop

Location: Northeast Mesa.

Distance: 5.3-mile loop.

Time: 1 hour.

Tread: Singletrack.

Aerobic level: Easy.

Technical difficulty: 3.

Hazards: Loose gravel in washes. This is a heavily used trail; watch for horses, hikers, and other riders.

Highlights: This is a fine, easy cruise of moderate length on singletrack. The Moon Rock Trail section is especially enjoyable as it zigzags through the cholla-cactus forest.

Land status: Usery Mountain Recreation Area, Tonto National Forest.

Maps: USGS Apache Junction.

Access: From Mesa, go north on Ellsworth Road, which

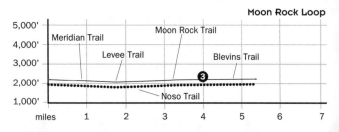

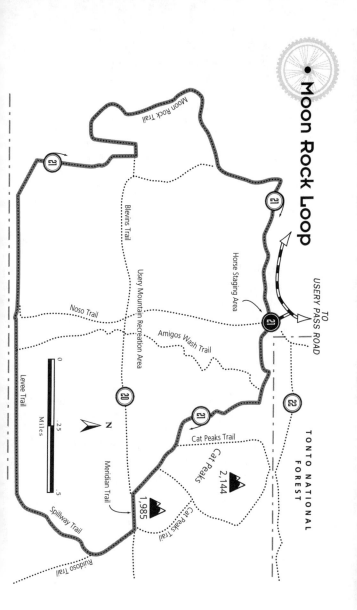

Moon Rock Loop

TO
USERY PASS ROAD

21

21

21

Moon Rock Trail

Moon Rock Trail

Blevins Trail

Usery Mountain Recreation Area

Noso Trail

Amigos Wash Trail

Horse Staging Area

21

Cat Peaks Trail

Cat Peaks

2,144

20

22

TONTO NATIONAL FOREST

Levee Trail

Meridian Trail

Cat Peaks Trail

1,985

Spillway Trail

Ruidoso Trail

N

Miles
0   .25   .5

becomes Usery Pass Road. Turn right at the park entrance and go to the horse staging area, which is the trailhead.

The ride

0.0   Ride smooth, easy singletrack, which is slightly downhill. Beginners may want to walk across a wash crossing near the start.

0.3   Continue straight past Amigos Wash Trail turnoff.

0.7   Cat Peaks Trail goes left; pedal straight ahead.

0.8   Cat Pass Trail goes left; continue straight ahead.

0.9   Go left on Meridian Trail, which runs straight east.

1.1   Ride past Cat Peaks Trail, then hang a right onto Spillway Trail.

1.3   Continue past Ruidoso Trail.

1.7   Turn right on Levee Trail, which oddly enough follows the top of a flood control levee to the west.

2.3   Continue past Noso Trail (this is a shortcut back to the trailhead, if needed).

2.8   Cross Crismon Wash Trail. The levee begins to curve right, then ends.

3.3   Levee Trail ends; go left on Moon Rock Trail, which curves left, then wanders through the desert before turning north, then east.

4.7   End of Moon Rock Trail; now pedal left on Blevins Trail.

5.3   End of the ride at the horse staging area.

Pass Mountain Trail

Location: Northeast Mesa.

Distance: 7.7-mile loop.

Time: 3 hours.

Tread: Singletrack.

Aerobic level: Moderate.

Technical difficulty: 3 and 4 with a short section of 5-.

Hazards: Parts of this trail are rocky and steep, and all but expert riders will want to walk several sections. The park does not recommend this trail for bicycles, though it is open. This is a heavily used trail, so watch for horses and hikers.

Highlights: This is a technically demanding loop with some very hard sections and a lot of smooth tread as well. It loops around the mountain east of the park and features great views.

Land status: Usery Mountain Recreation Area, Tonto National Forest.

Maps: USGS Apache Junction.

Access: From Mesa, go north on Ellsworth Road, which becomes Usery Pass Road. Turn right at the park entrance and go to the horse staging area, which is the trailhead.

• Pass Mountain Trail

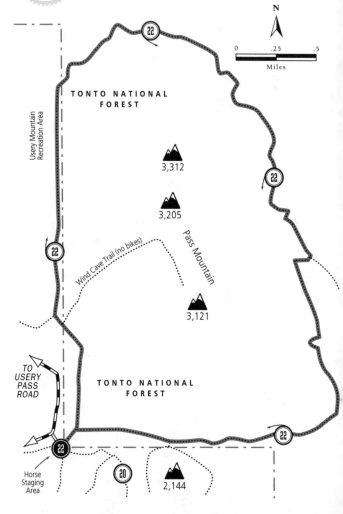

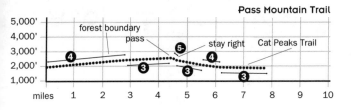

The ride

0.0   Ride east on the Pass Mountain Trail.

0.1   Hang a left at the T intersection.

0.7   Pass Wind Cave Trail, which is closed to bikes. Numerous rock water bars and rocky wash crossings make this section challenging.

2.3   Go through a gate onto the Tonto National Forest. You'll start to climb gradually around the north side of the mountain, and the tread becomes much smoother.

2.8   Cross a ridge. The Goldfield Mountains are visible to the northeast, and beyond, Four Peaks.

4.4   Cross a pass (the high point of the ride) and start a steep, rocky, eroded descent. Most riders will want to walk.

4.6   Be sure to stay right here, to remain on the new trail. You'll curve around a rock outcrop as the trail becomes nearly smooth and starts a gradual descent.

5.4   The trail steepens and becomes rocky again.

6.1   Ignore an unsigned trail branching left and continue straight as the trail swings westward around the base of the mountain.

7.1   Pass the junction with Cat Peaks Trail.

7.6   Turn left at the T intersection.

7.7   End of the ride at the horse staging area.

Mazatzal Mountains

Doll Baby Ranch

Location: About 5 miles east of Payson.

Distance: 12 miles out and back.

Time: 3 hours.

Tread: 12 miles maintained dirt road.

Aerobic level: Moderate.

Technical difficulty: 2.

Hazards: Occasional deep ruts; a few rocky sections.

Highlights: This is an especially scenic ride through pinyon–juniper forest to the East Verde River, a small stream lined with Arizona sycamores.

Land status: Tonto National Forest; private.

Maps: USGS North Peak; Tonto National Forest.

Access: From Payson on Arizona Highway 87, drive west on Main Street. Stay on the main road past a golf course, where the pavement ends and the road becomes Forest Road 406. Continue to the junction with the Cypress Thicket Road, FR 414, which is 5.2 miles from AZ 87. Park here.

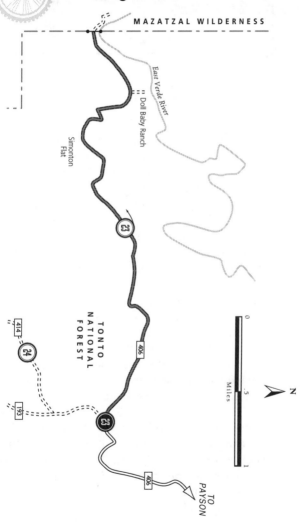

Doll Baby Ranch

MAZATZAL WILDERNESS

East Verde River

Doll Baby Ranch

Simonton Flat

23

406

TONTO NATIONAL FOREST

414

24

193

23

406

TO PAYSON

N

Miles
0 .5 1

The ride

0.0 Ride west on FR 406 as the road continues downhill toward the north end of the Mazatzal Mountains.

1.4 The descent moderates and the terrain becomes more open in chaparral brush.

1.9 Cross a wash and ride up a moderately steep hill.

3.6 Cross another wash and climb a short, steep hill.

4.3 Cross a cattle guard onto private land. From this point to the end of the ride, stay on the road to avoid trespassing. Cross Simonton Flat, then climb a steep, rocky hill.

4.5 Start down a rocky section.

4.8 Pass the City Creek Trailhead as the road levels out along the river bottom.

5.1 Doll Baby Ranch on the right.

6.0 The locked gate is the turnaround point. (The road beyond the gate enters the Mazatzal Wilderness and is closed to bikes and all vehicles except by permission from the USDA Forest Service.) The Arizona sycamores bordering the East Verde River make this a delightful spot. Like many Arizona rivers, the East Verde is usually a small creek. At times, such as after a thunderstorm or during spring snowmelt, it can be a major torrent.

12.0 Back at the trailhead.

Cypress Thicket

Location: About 5 miles west of Payson.

Distance: 28.8 miles out and back; 14.4 miles one way with a shuttle.

Time: 3 hours.

Tread: Doubletrack.

Aerobic level: Moderate.

Technical difficulty: 2+.

Hazards: There are a few rocky sections, and the road is usually rutted. Don't attempt this ride after snow or rain—it will be very muddy.

Highlights: A fine cruise through a beautiful Arizona cypress forest through the foothills of the Mazatzal Mountains. The entire ride can be done with a car shuttle, or you can turn around at Mineral Creek Trailhead for an out-and-back ride of 10.2 miles, which will take 2 hours.

Land status: Tonto National Forest.

Maps: USGS North Peak, Gisela, Mazatzal Peak, Payson South; Tonto National Forest.

Access: Unless you do the ride as an out and back, you'll need to leave a vehicle at the end of the ride. When approaching from the south on Arizona Highway 87, turn left (west) onto Forest Road 414 just north of the hamlet of Rye. (This turnoff is about 9 miles south of Payson.) To reach the start

• Cypress Thicket

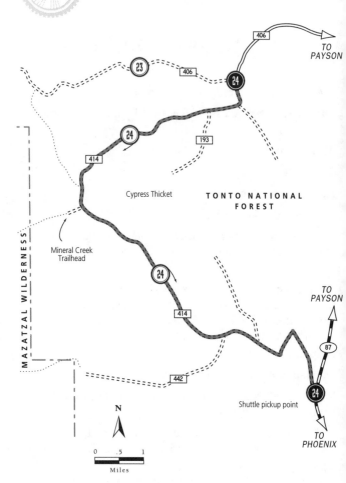

of the ride, continue to Payson on AZ 87, then turn left (west) on Main Street at a traffic light. Stay on the main road past a golf course, where the pavement ends and the road becomes FR 406. Continue to the junction with the Cypress Thicket Road, FR 414, which is 5.2 miles from AZ 87. Park here.

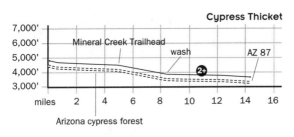

The ride

0.0 Go left on FR 414 to start the ride. You'll generally be descending, but it's a roller coaster.

0.7 Bear right to stay on FR 414, the main road. Although you are still descending, there are some short uphill sections.

1.5 Ride straight ahead to remain on FR 414.

3.4 Here, you'll ride into an especially fine Arizona cypress forest. They're the trees with the curly red bark, found only in central Arizona.

5.1 Pedal straight ahead at the turnoff to Mineral Creek Trailhead. (If you want to make the trailhead your destination for an out-and-back ride, turn right and go 0.2 miles to the parking area. The junipers and cypresses provide shade, and there are good views of North Peak and the eastern slopes of the Mazatzal Mountains.)

6.7 Cross a (normally dry) wash.

7.7	Cross the same wash again.
8.5	This time, when you cross the wash, the road stays on the right bank for a while.
10.8	Ride across the wash again, then go straight at a cross-roads, to stay on FR 414.
11.3	Pedal up a hill.
12.3	Turn right at a T intersection to stay on FR 414.
14.4	AZ 87 is on the left; this is either your shuttle pickup point or your turnaround point.
28.8	Back at the trailhead.

Mount Peeley Road

Location: 51 miles northeast of Mesa.

Distance: 17 miles out and back.

Time: 3 hours.

Tread: Seldom-maintained dirt road.

Aerobic level: Strenuous.

Technical difficulty: 2.

Hazards: A few rocks and some rocky sections; occasional vehicle traffic on weekends. The first 6 miles are hot in summer. Keep your speed down on the downhill return.

Highlights: This narrow road climbs along a high ridgeline in the Mazatzal Mountains with great views. The last section winds through a cool pine-and-fir forest.

• Mount Peeley Road

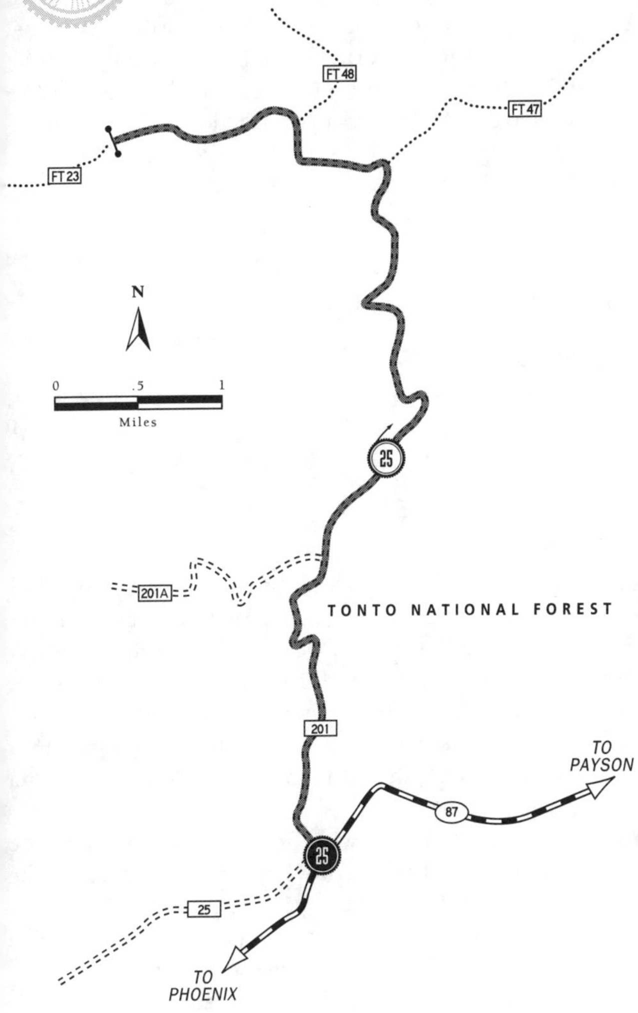

FT 48

FT 47

FT 23

N

0   .5   1
Miles

25

201A

TONTO NATIONAL FOREST

201

TO
PAYSON

25

87

25

TO
PHOENIX

Land status: Tonto National Forest.

Maps: Reno Pass, Mazatzal Peak USGS; Tonto National Forest.

Access: From Mesa, drive about 51 miles north on Arizona Highway 87 to Slate Creek Divide on the crest of the Mazatzal Mountains, then turn left onto Forest Road 201 and park. (This section of AZ 87 is under construction and access to FR 201 may change. Check with the Tonto National Forest for updates.)

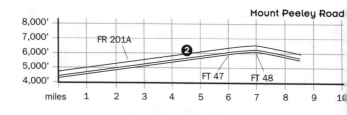

The ride

0.0   Crank up the steep climb (if you are going downhill you're on the wrong road). Steep climbs alternate with short descents as the road climbs onto the ridge.

2.4   Pass the junction with FR 201A; stay on the main road, FR 201. There are several side roads that are interesting to explore. As you climb, you'll pass into chaparral brush and then encounter a few Arizona cypress trees.

6.0   Pass the junction with Forest Trail 47, where the climb ends. The road now swings west and skirts the north slopes of a ridge, passing through cool, shady stands of ponderosa pine and Douglas-fir. (The Mazatzal Wilderness, which is closed to bicycles, lies about half a mile north of this road.)

7.0	The high point of the ride at the junction with FT 48. Cruise down through open areas of chaparral with fine views of Mount Peeley to the west and Mazatzal Peak, the highest in the range, to the north.
8.5	Mount Peeley Trailhead and the turnaround point. (The trails beyond this point enter the Mazatzal Wilderness and are closed to bikes.)
17.0	Back at the trailhead.

Option: At mile 6.0, turn right onto FT 47. You can ride this old road about half a mile north through the forest to the wilderness boundary. If you want some great views of the Mazatzal Mountains, leave your bike near the base of the first rock outcropping on the right and scramble up to the top via the west side. This option is doubletrack, aerobically easy, technically rated 2, and adds 1 mile to the ride.

Slate Creek Divide

Location: 51 miles northeast of Mesa.

Distance: 10.6-mile loop.

Time: 3 hours.

Tread: 5.1 miles maintained dirt road; 5.5 miles doubletrack.

Aerobic level: Strenuous.

Technical difficulty: 2 on maintained dirt road; 3+ on doubletrack.

• Slate Creek Divide

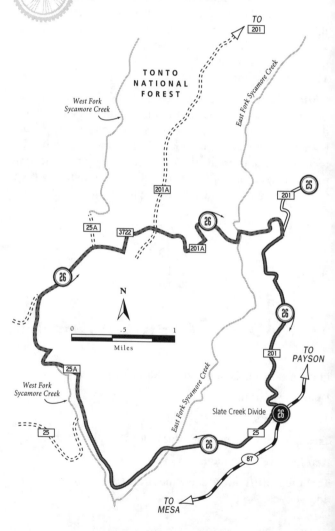

Hazards: Watch for oncoming traffic on Forest Roads 201 and 25; keep your speed down. There are rocky, loose sections on the doubletrack, and areas of loose gravel on the maintained dirt road.

Highlights: This scenic loop in the Mazatzal Mountains combines smooth ridge running with an enjoyable section along the West Fork of Sycamore Creek. The creek flows intermittently through groves of Arizona sycamore, and the pools along the creek are tempting on a hot day.

Land status: Tonto National Forest.

Maps: USGS Reno Pass; Tonto National Forest.

Access: From Mesa, drive about 51 miles north on Arizona Highway 87 to Slate Creek Divide on the crest of the Mazatzal Mountains, then turn left onto FR 201 and park. (This section of AZ 87 is under construction and access to FR 201 may change. Check with the Tonto National Forest for updates.)

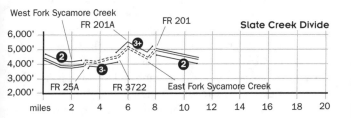

The ride

0.0 Go left, downhill, onto FR 25, an occasionally maintained dirt road. Roll down a moderate descent to the southwest, almost parallel to the highway.

1.3	Cross the East Fork of Sycamore Creek. Now the descent levels out as the road parallels the creek. The creek flows seasonally. In dry periods there'll be just a few pools.
2.0	Turn sharply right as the road meets the West Fork of Sycamore Creek and starts climbing gradually northward.
2.7	Ride straight onto FR 25A, which is doubletrack and continues north on the right side of the creek. Crank up a steep, short climb as the road leaves the creek for a stretch.
3.0	The road levels out and contours along the steep canyon wall.
3.6	Cross the creek. This section of the creek seems to have more water than the East Fork, and it's a delight to ride alongside the tinkling mountain stream. There are a few rocky places, though.
4.4	Pass the spur road to Sunflower Mine and continue straight on FR 25A.
5.0	The doubletrack spends some time right in the creek bed, and it becomes very rocky in places.
5.3	Turn right onto FR 3722 and grunt up a very steep hill, climbing east, out of the creek. After a bit the climb moderates somewhat.
6.1	You're at the top of the climb and the high point of the ride at a crossroads. Go straight onto FR 201A, which immediately starts descending steeply into the East Fork of Sycamore Creek. (FR 201A also goes left here—see the optional ride.)
7.5	Roll across the East Fork and start a steep climb up the east side of the canyon.
8.2	Turn right onto FR 201, the Mount Peeley Road, which is maintained dirt. Except for a couple of short climbs, it's all downhill from here.
10.6	AZ 87 and the end of the ride.

Options: At the high point of the ride, you could turn left onto FR 201A and take this doubletrack north along the ridge between the east and west forks of Sycamore Canyon. It's 2.8 miles to FR 201, the Mount Peeley Road, which is maintained dirt. Turn right here and follow FR 201 east, then south to AZ 87 and your vehicle. See the Mount Peeley ride for more details. This option adds 7 miles and 680 feet of climbing to the loop.

Cottonwood Camp

Location: About 30 miles northeast of Mesa.

Distance: 12.8 miles out and back.

Time: 3 hours.

Tread: Maintained dirt road.

Aerobic level: Moderate (easy with a shuttle).

Technical difficulty: 2.

Hazards: Loose gravel; occasional ruts. This ride is downhill on the way out, so allow plenty of time for the slower climb back to your vehicle. As an option, you could do a car shuttle and ride one way.

Highlights: This mostly smooth dirt road is an easy cruise through the rolling foothills of the Mazatzal Mountains.

Land status: Tonto National Forest.

• Cottonwood Camp

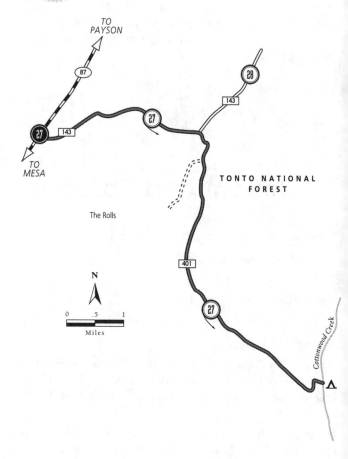

TO
PAYSON

87

28

143

27

27   143

TO
MESA

TONTO NATIONAL
FOREST

The Rolls

401

N

0   .5   1
Miles

27

Cottonwood Creek

Δ

Maps: USGS Mine Mountain, Mormon Flat Dam, Adams Mesa; Tonto National Forest.

Access: From Mesa, drive north on Arizona Highway 87. Note your mileage at the junction with Shea Boulevard and drive 14 miles farther to the start at the junction with Forest Road 143, on the right.

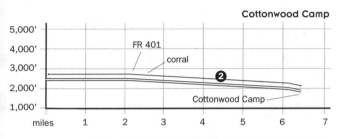

The ride

0.0   Ride east on FR 143, which wanders east through the open desert.

2.1   Hang a right onto FR 401 and roll down a gradual descent as the road heads generally south.

2.6   Bear left at a corral to stay on FR 401.

6.2   Start down a short, steep hill.

6.4   Cottonwood Camp, located next to Cottonwood Wash, and the turnaround point. Now used mainly by recreational campers, this spot used to be a cowboys' line camp. Ranch hands used line camps as overnight stops or temporary bases while rounding up cattle or working in the area. (The area east of Cottonwood Wash, with the exception of Cane Springs Road, is in the Four Peaks Wilderness Area and is closed to bikes.)

12.8   Back at the trailhead.

Options: Using the ride directions, shuttle a vehicle to the end of the ride, then return to the start to ride it one way, downhill.

99

Four Peaks

Location: About 30 miles northeast of Mesa.

Distance: 36.6 miles out and back.

Time: 7 hours.

Tread: 13.4 miles maintained dirt road; 23.2 miles doubletrack.

Aerobic level: Strenuous.

Technical difficulty: 2 on maintained dirt road; 2+ on doubletrack.

Hazards: Frequent deep ruts and gullies and a few rocky sections on the doubletrack. This is a very long ride with a lot of climbing. For riders in seriously good shape only! The rest of us should consider the easier options at the end of the description.

Highlights: This long route passes through a picturesque section of Sonoran desert, a rugged landscape of granite boulders and saguaro cactus, and ends on the crest of the Mazatzal Mountains.

Land status: Tonto National Forest.

Maps: USGS Adams Mesa, Mine Mountain, Four Peaks; Tonto National Forest.

Access: From Mesa, drive north on Arizona Highway 87. Note your mileage at the junction with Shea Boulevard and

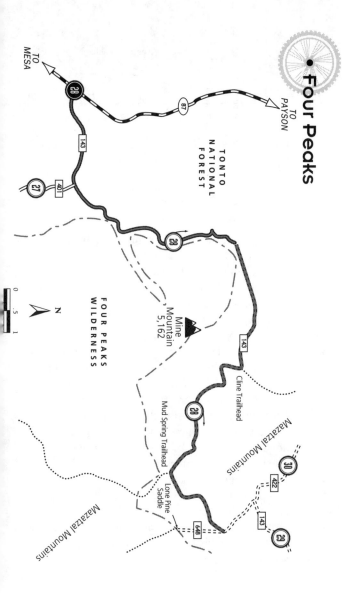

Four Peaks

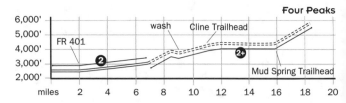

drive 14 miles farther to the junction with Forest Road 143 on the right. This is where the ride starts.

The ride

0.0   Cruise down the smooth, maintained dirt road to the east, FR 143.

2.1   Pedal left at the junction with FR 401, and start a rolling, gradual climb through the desert. The Four Peaks Wilderness, which is closed to bikes, borders the road to the west and south beyond this point.

4.1   Bear left, to stay on FR 143, the main road.

6.7   Now, the road steepens and becomes narrower as you start around the north side of Mine Mountain. Road maintenance is very infrequent, so watch for washouts and gullies in the road surface.

8.7   Cross a ridge and start to descend. You've been riding through classic Sonoran desert up to this point, but now the giant saguaros start to give way to chaparral brush and juniper trees.

9.1   Start climbing again.

10.1   Cross a wash.

11.2   Pass by Cline Trailhead.

11.8   Ride across a pass. You might want to stop and check out the rugged basin you'll be crossing next.

15.4   Ride past Mud Spring Trailhead, up a rocky section, and start the final, steep climb. (The trails south of this trailhead are in the Four Peaks Wilderness and are closed to bikes.)

18.3   The Mazatzal crest and the turnaround point (or the end of the ride if you have a shuttle vehicle waiting). If you still have some energy left, you can turn right onto FR 648 and ride another 1.4 miles to Lone Pine Saddle. (The Four Peaks Wilderness starts at Lone Pine Saddle, and the trails beyond this point are closed to bikes.)

36.6   Back at the trailhead.

Options: Those desiring an easy ride can turn around at the 2.1 mile point (the junction with FR 401). This is a great cruise through beautiful desert, suitable for families and beginners. For a more challenging ride, continue to the start of the steep climb at 6.7 miles before turning back. If you can arrange a shuttle to the top of the climb, you can do this ride in reverse, one way, which is mostly, but not entirely, downhill.

El Oso Road

Location: About 85 miles northeast of Mesa.

Distance: 22.6 miles out and back.

Time: 5 hours.

Tread: Doubletrack.

Aerobic level: Strenuous.

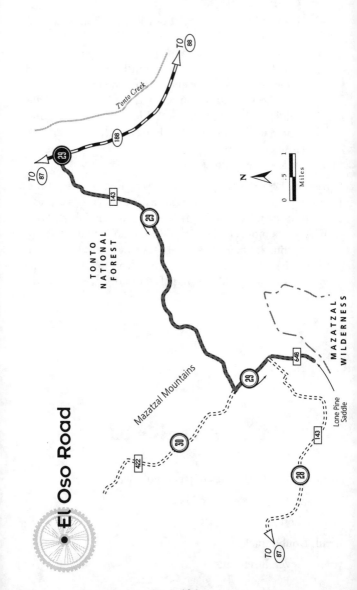

El Oso Road

TO 88

Tonto Creek

188

29

TO 87

143

29

TONTO
NATIONAL
FOREST

N

0 .5 1
Miles

MAZATZAL
WILDERNESS

Mazatzal Mountains

648

Lone Pine
Saddle

29

30

143

422

28

TO 87

Technical difficulty: 2.

Hazards: Occasional rocky or rutted areas; traffic on weekends.

Highlights: A thigh-burning climb up a scenic ridge on the east slopes of the Mazatzal Mountains. You'll start in saguaro-studded Sonoran desert and end up in ponderosa pine forest.

Land status: Tonto National Forest.

Maps: USGS Tonto Basin, Four Peaks; Tonto National Forest.

Access: From Mesa, drive north on Arizona Highway 87. Note your mileage at the junction with Shea Boulevard. Continue another 48 miles, then turn right onto AZ 188. Continue about 20 miles to El Oso Road (Forest Road 143) and park on the right. To shuttle riders to the top of the ride, follow the ride directions.

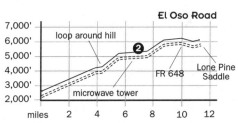

The ride

0.0 The dirt road, FR 143, starts climbing immediately and continuously, with very few breaks. Of course, you can ride up as far as you like, then turn around for a bomber descent. Just watch for oncoming traffic, especially on weekends. As you start to climb, you pass through Sonoran desert, with its distinctive giant saguaro cactus. Unlike many other doubletracks in the Four Peaks area, the road surface is fairly smooth and rut free.

3.8 Whew! The climb moderates for a bit.

4.3 Gear down—it gets steeper.

4.5 Crank around a sharp switchback to the right. To the left, the road loops around a hill for those vehicles unable to make the sharp turn. You shouldn't have that problem, but you might want to check out the view.

5.6 Another break from the climb.

7.5 As the road steepens once more, notice the tall ponderosa pines that are starting to appear in the hollows and north-facing slopes.

8.8 Pass a microwave tower, then turn left to stay on FR 143. You've done nearly all the climb—now cruise south along the ridge toward Four Peaks, visible ahead.

9.9 Turn left on FR 648, and head toward Lone Pine Saddle.

10.8 Pass Pigeon Trailhead (this is a wilderness trail that's closed to bikes).

11.3 Lone Pine Saddle Trailhead and the turnaround. The trails leading out of this trailhead go into Four Peaks Wilderness, which is closed to bicycles. On the slopes above are thousands of burned trees, mute evidence of the 60,000-acre Lone Fire that burned most of the area in 1995. Despite the intensity of the fires, many pockets of pines and other vegetation survived, such as the area just above the trailhead. Even in the heavily burned areas, Gambel oaks are already growing from the roots of their burnt ancestors, and the hillsides are covered with flowers during the summer rainy season.

22.6 Back at the trailhead.

Options: Talk someone into shuttling you to the top for a thrilling downhill-only ride.

Little Pine Flat

Location: About 50 miles northeast of Mesa.

Distance: 13.4 miles out and back.

Time: 3 hours.

Tread: Doubletrack.

Aerobic level: Moderate.

Technical difficulty: 3-.

Hazards: Numerous rocks and ruts; some ledges.

Highlights: This ride follows the northern extension of El Oso Road along the crest of the Mazatzal Mountains. You'll get stunning views clear across the Phoenix valley to the southwest and of the Sierra Ancha and the Mogollon Rim to the east and northeast. And the riding's fun, too!

Land status: Tonto National Forest.

Maps: USGS Four Peaks, Boulder Mountain, Tonto Basin; Tonto National Forest.

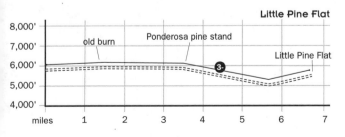

• Little Pine Flat

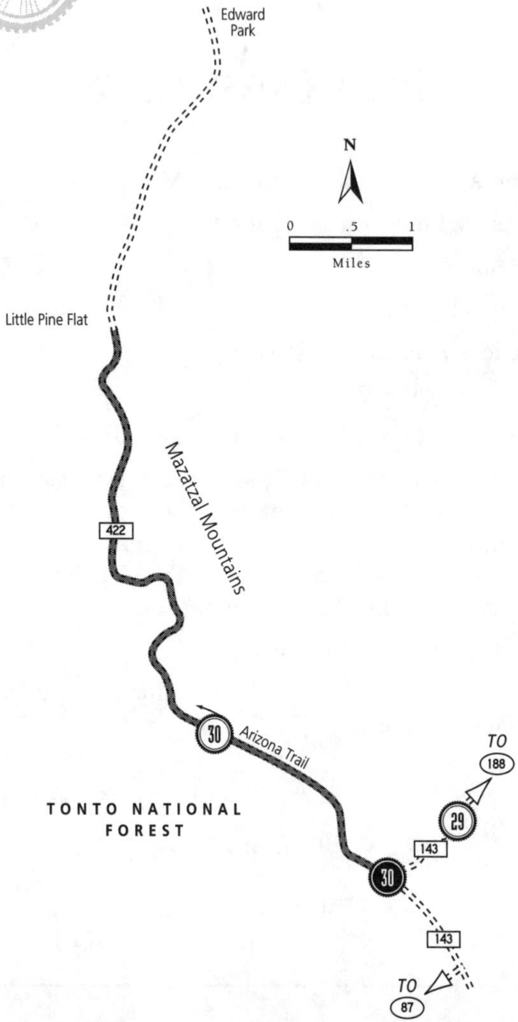

Edward
Park

N

0   .5   1
Miles

Little Pine Flat

Mazatzal Mountains

422

30 Arizona Trail

TONTO NATIONAL
FOREST

TO
188

29

143

30

143

TO
87

Access: From Mesa, drive north on Arizona Highway 87. Note your mileage at the junction with Shea Boulevard and drive 14 miles farther, then turn right on Forest Road 143. Go 19.4 miles on this slow, winding dirt road, and park at the junction with FR 422. (Parking at the junction itself is limited; you'll find more parking spots just up FR 422.) As an alternate approach, see the Four Peaks East ride to approach from the eastern side via AZ 188—though longer overall, the dirt road portion is shorter and smoother.

The ride

0.0   The doubletrack winds north along the Mazatzal crest, going up and down small hills. Here the scenery is so good that this section was picked for a passage of the Arizona Trail, a route that crosses the state from Utah to Mexico.

0.3   Bear left to stay on FR 422, the main road.

1.6   Roll down a short, steep descent through granite boulders and recently burned forest and brush. These mountains have had numerous large forest fires in past years, probably because they are relatively dry and get pounded by lightning strikes each summer.

3.5   Stay right at a clearing to stay on FR 422, which is the main road. You'll soon start downhill through an extensive stand of pines as the road swings around the north side of a hill.

5.2   The descent moderates as you roll though chaparral brush along the main ridge.

5.7   Start up a gradual climb.

6.7   Roll into a stand of pines at Little Pine Flat. This shady patch of trees is a good place to turn around. Adventurous (and tireless) riders can follow the road north several more miles to its end at Edward Park, but it becomes badly eroded and very steep a short distance north of Little Pine Flat.

13.4   Back at the trailhead.

Rock Creek

Location: About 89 miles northeast of Mesa.

Distance: 6.8 miles out and back.

Time: 1.5 hours.

Tread: 1.6 miles maintained dirt road; 5.2 miles doubletrack.

Aerobic level: Easy.

Technical difficulty: 2.

Hazards: Some loose gravel and a few deep ruts and rocky spots.

Highlights: This is an easy ride to a shady desert stream. This is a great ride for beginners and families—and fit riders who want a nice cruise.

Land status: Tonto National Forest.

Maps: USGS Theodore Roosevelt Dam, Four Peaks; Tonto National Forest.

Access: From Mesa, drive north on Arizona

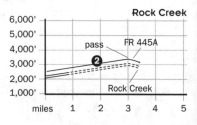

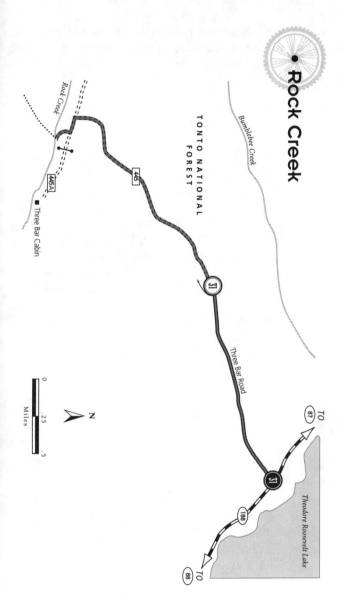

Rock Creek

Rock Creek

Three Bar Cabin

TONTO NATIONAL
FOREST

Bumblebee Creek

445A

445

31

Three Bar Road

31

188

TO
87

TO
88

Theodore Roosevelt Lake

N

0   .25   .5
Miles

Highway 87. Note your mileage at the junction with Shea
Boulevard. Continue another 48 miles, then turn right on AZ
188. Continue about 24 miles to Three Bar Road, Forest Road
445, and park on the right.

The ride

0.0	Pedal up the smooth dirt road to the west as it climbs gradually up a canyon.
0.8	The road gets rougher but the climbing is still easy.
3.0	Stay right at an unsigned junction and ride over a broad pass into the Rock Creek drainage.
3.2	Turn left onto FR 445A at a T intersection.
3.3	Turn right at the sign for Rock Creek Trailhead.
3.4	Turn around at the banks of Rock Creek, a seasonal desert stream shaded with graceful Arizona sycamore trees.
6.8	Back at the trailhead.

Superstition Mountains

Apache Trail

Location: About 25 miles east of Apache Junction.

Distance: 21.5 miles one way with a shuttle.

Time: 4 hours.

Tread: Maintained dirt road.

Aerobic level: Strenuous.

Technical difficulty: 2.

Hazards: Loose gravel. This is a very popular scenic drive. Be alert for heavy traffic, including vehicles with boat trailers, and keep your speed under control at all times. Be especially careful on blind curves.

Highlights: The historic Apache Trail Road winds along the northern reaches of the Superstition Mountains to Theodore Roosevelt Dam, the first large-scale federal reclamation project. Built at the turn of the century, the road was the only access to the remote dam site. Today, two more reservoirs, Canyon Lake and Apache Lake, fill the former Salt River Canyon and form the northern border of the Superstition Mountains. Though the ride is long, the scenery is great and the road surface is smooth.

Land status: Tonto National Forest.

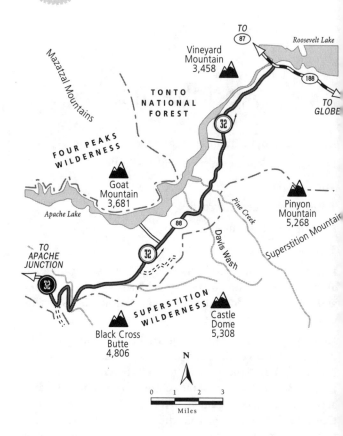

• Apache Trail

Mazatzal Mountains

TO
87

Roosevelt Lake

Vineyard
Mountain
3,458

TONTO
NATIONAL
FOREST

188

TO
GLOBE

32

FOUR PEAKS
WILDERNESS

Goat
Mountain
3,681

Apache Lake

88

Pine Creek

Pinyon
Mountain
5,268

Superstition Mountain

Davis Wash

32

TO
APACHE
JUNCTION

32

SUPERSTITION
WILDERNESS

Castle
Dome
5,308

Black Cross
Butte
4,806

N

0   1   2   3
Miles

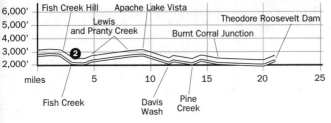

Maps: USGS Horse Mesa Dam, Pinyon Mountain, Theodore Roosevelt Dam; Tonto National Forest.

Access: This ride requires a shuttle, which is best done by talking someone into dropping you off at the start, then having them act as a sag wagon, following the last rider to the end of the ride. To reach the start from Phoenix, drive east on the Superstition Freeway (U.S. Highway 60), then exit onto Arizona Highway 88 (Apache Trail) at Apache Junction. Continue 24.6 miles east, past Canyon Lake and Tortilla Flat, to the end of the pavement. Park on the right.

The ride

0.0   Pedal across the broad expanse of Horse Mesa, following the road as it winds through the rugged terrain, climbing gradually.

0.9   Pass the Tortilla Trailhead turnoff.

1.8   Horse Mesa abruptly ends at the impressive descent called Fish Creek Hill. The road is narrow here—keep your speed down and watch for uphill traffic on the blind curves. There are places where running off the road will get you some big air of the worst kind.

3.5   Roll across the bridge over Fish Creek. There's a small pullout where you can stop to check out this most impressive canyon.

4.4	Start a long climb up Lewis and Pranty Creek.
4.7	Cross a bridge and crank past a highway maintenance yard.
7.9	The climb moderates a bit.
9.1	Whew! The road levels off as you pass Apache Lake Vista. The lake, formed by Horse Mesa Dam, backs up right to the base of Roosevelt Dam. Apache Lake will be to your left for the rest of the ride, though not always in sight.
11.3	Resume the climb.
11.6	Roll across the bridge at Davis Wash.
12.1	Finally, start a descent.
13.4	Cross the bridge at Pine Creek, which is usually flowing. Pine trees? Where? Well, the creek actually starts high in the eastern Superstition Mountains in a fine stand of ponderosa pines. Oh yeah—start climbing again.
14.7	Top of the hill; cruise down a long hill.
15.9	Pedal past the turnoff to Burnt Corral Campground. Now the road narrows and does a series of short climbs and descents as it works its way along the precipitous shore of Apache Lake.
20.2	Start up the final climb from Apache Lake.
20.4	Roll onto pavement. Use caution, because the road is still narrow, and there are more bad big-air opportunities.
21.5	Roll past Roosevelt Dam to a viewpoint on the left and the end of the ride. It's hard to believe, but all the construction trucks and other traffic needed to build the dam came up the road you just rode. Completed in 1911, the original dam was constructed of stone blocks quarried on site. In 1996, the dam was raised to 357 feet to provide flood storage in the lake, and the old structure was reinforced by covering it with concrete. The highway along the south and west

shores was rebuilt above the new lake level, and the massive arch bridge was built to carry traffic across the mouth of the canyon in front of the dam.

Queen Creek

Location: About 20 miles east of Apache Junction.

Distance: 16.4 miles out and back.

Time: 2 hours.

Tread: Maintained dirt road.

Aerobic level: Easy.

Technical difficulty: 2-.

Hazards: Occasional loose gravel.

Highlights: This is an easy ride that follows Queen Creek Wash through the foothills of the Superstition Mountains. It's even easier if you do it in reverse, one way, by leaving a shuttle vehicle at the Queen Creek turnoff.

Land status: Tonto National Forest; private.

Maps: USGS Florence Junction, Picketpost Mountain; Tonto National Forest.

Access: From Apache Junction, drive about 18 miles east on U.S. Highway 60, then turn left on the Queen Creek Road. Follow this paved road 1.9 miles, then turn right on Forest Road 357, a maintained dirt road, and park. To do the ride

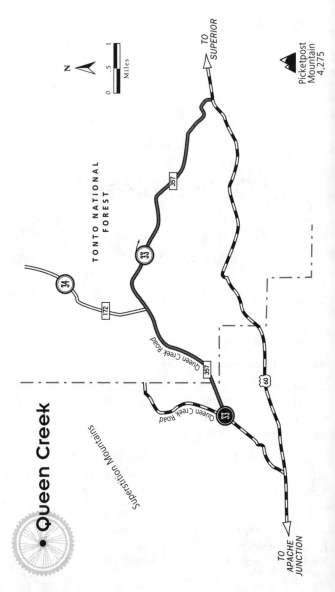

Queen Creek

TONTO NATIONAL FOREST

Superstition Mountains

TO SUPERIOR

Picketpost Mountain
4,275

Queen Creek Road

Queen Creek Road

TO APACHE JUNCTION

N

0 .5 1
Miles

34

172

33

357

357

33

60

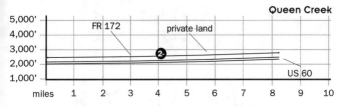

one way in reverse, leave a vehicle here, return to US 60, turn left, and go about 8 miles to the east end of Queen Creek Road.

The ride

0.0 Ride east on the broad, smooth road. Queen Creek, though lined with water-loving trees, is usually a dry wash. The main attraction of this ride is the scenery.

3.1 Pass the junction with FR 172 on the left; roll straight ahead.

5.6 Ride onto private land; the road surface becomes a little rougher because it was badly paved at one time.

8.2 US 60 and the turnaround point. If you have time, check out the Boyce Thompson Arboretum a couple of miles east on the highway. It has a great collection of desert plants and a fine walk along water with graceful trees. There is a picnic area as well.

16.4 Back at the trailhead.

Woodbury Road

Location: About 25 miles east of Apache Junction.

Distance: 28 miles out and back.

Time: 5 hours.

Tread: Maintained dirt road.

Aerobic level: Strenuous.

Technical difficulty: 2.

Hazards: A few rocky places on road; occasional loose gravel, especially in wash crossings. This is a very long ride in remote country; be prepared with extra water, clothing, food, and tools.

Highlights: A long, but scenic, ride through a spectacular canyon in the Superstition Mountains. All of this ride is worth doing, but keep in mind that you can turn around at any point.

Land status: Tonto National Forest.

Maps: USGS Picketpost Mountain, Iron Mountain; Tonto National Forest.

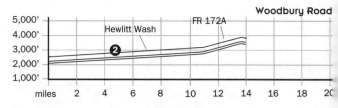

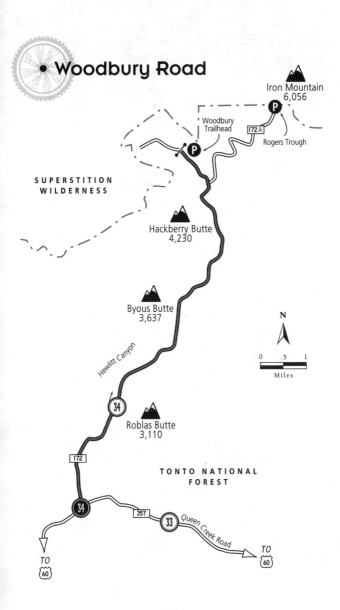

Woodbury Road

Iron Mountain
6,056

P

Woodbury
Trailhead

172 A

Rogers Trough

P

SUPERSTITION
WILDERNESS

Hackberry Butte
4,230

Byous Butte
3,637

N

0   .5   1

Miles

Hewitt Canyon

34

Roblas Butte
3,110

172

TONTO NATIONAL
FOREST

34

357

33

Queen Creek Road

TO
60

TO
60

Access: From Apache Junction, go about 18 miles east on U.S. Highway 60, then turn left on the Queen Creek Road. Follow this paved road 1.9 miles, then turn right on Forest Road 357, a maintained dirt road. Continue 3.1 miles to the junction with FR 172, which is on the left, and park.

The ride

0.0 Ride across Queen Creek, which is normally dry, then continue north on FR 172 as it winds through the Superstition foothills.

3.6 Stay right and cross a cattleguard to stay on FR 172.

6.7 The road drops into and follows Hewlitt Wash for a short distance.

9.3 Rattle down a short, rocky descent.

11.2 Notice that the rugged, craggy mountainsides are giving way to a more rounded look. This is because the bedrock has changed from volcanic to granitic. This particular granite weathers easily, giving the hills their rounded look. You'll also see the scar from an old fire on the left side of the road. Now, the road starts to climb more steeply.

12.5 Stay left at the junction with FR 172A.

13.7 Hang a sharp right at a locked gate, and roll down a short hill to the Woodbury Trailhead.

14.0 Turn around at the Superstition Wilderness boundary. This is a wild and remote-feeling spot, entirely surrounded by rugged mountains.

28.0 Back at the trailhead.

Options: If you want a real workout, you can ride FR 172A from the 12.5 mile point to the Rogers Trough Trailhead, a distance of 4.0 miles. This makes the total out-and-back distance 33.0 miles.

12.5 Turn right onto FR 172A, and start a relentless climb on this infrequently maintained dirt road.

14.1 Notice, between puffs, that the saguaro cactus is giving way to juniper trees and a kind of scrubby grassland.

16.1 Top of the climb, whew! Hang a sharp left and rattle down a somewhat rocky wash.

16.5 Rogers Trough, the wilderness boundary, and the end of the ride. This area, dominated by the bulk of Iron Mountain, is covered by a mixture of pinyon pines, juniper trees, and chaparral brush—quite a contrast to the Hewlitt Canyon area a few miles back down the road.

33.0 Back at the trailhead.

White Canyon

Location: About 42 miles east of Apache Junction.

Distance: 9.4 miles out and back.

Time: 2 hours.

Tread: 5.4 miles doubletrack, 4.0 miles maintained dirt road.

Aerobic level: Strenuous.

Technical difficulty: 2 on maintained dirt road, 2+ on doubletrack.

Hazards: Loose gravel, especially in wash crossings. Also watch for occasional deep ruts crosswise to the roads.

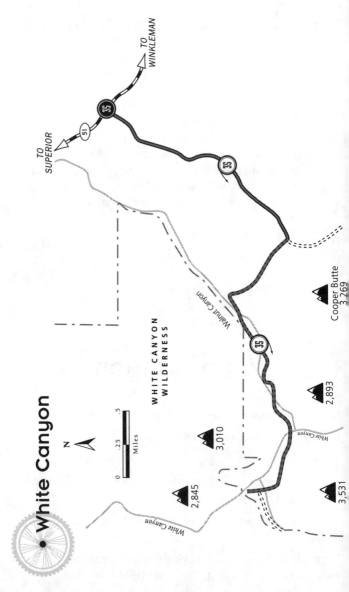

White Canyon

N

TO SUPERIOR

TO WINKLEMAN

51

35

35

35

35

WHITE CANYON WILDERNESS

Miles
0   .25   .5

Walnut Canyon

White Canyon

White Canyon

Cooper Butte
3,269

2,893

3,531

3,010

2,845

Highlights: The disadvantage of this ride is that it's downhill on the way in, and a long climb on the return. This is offset by the dramatic setting of deep canyons and jagged desert peaks.

Land status: Bureau of Land Management.

Maps: USGS Teapot Mountain.

Access: From Apache Junction, go about 32 miles east on U.S. Highway 60 to Superior, then turn right on Arizona Highway 177. Continue 9.7 miles to an unmarked, maintained dirt road on the right known locally as White Canyon Road. Park here.

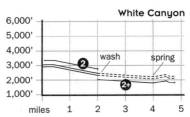

The ride

0.0	Roll down a hill, then start a short, easy climb.
0.4	Cross a pass and resume the descent.
2.0	Pedal right onto a doubletrack that goes down the wash.
4.0	A short spur road goes left to a spring at White Canyon; stay right as the road crosses the wash to its west side.
4.5	Top of a short, steep climb and start of an equally short, steep descent.
4.6	Hang a right.
4.7	Turn around at the White Canyon Wilderness boundary. If you have a bike lock, you can explore this remote, rugged canyon on foot for a way before you head back the way you came.
9.4	Back at the trailhead.

Appendix

Information Sources

Government Offices

City
Phoenix Mountains Preserve, 17642 N. 40th St., Phoenix, AZ 85032, (602) 262-7901.

South Mountain Park, 10919 S. Central Ave., Phoenix, AZ 85040-8302, (602) 495-0222.

County
Maricopa County Parks and Recreation Department, 3475 W. Durango St., Phoenix, AZ 85009, (602) 506-2930.

Cave Creek Recreation Area, 37019 N. Lava Lane, Phoenix, AZ 85027, (623) 465-0431.

Estrella Mountain Regional Park, 14805 West Vineyard Avenue, Goodyear, AZ 85338; (623) 932-3811.

McDowell Mountain Regional Park, Box 18415, Fountain Hills, AZ 85269, (480) 471-0173.

Usery Mountain Recreation Area, 3939 N. Usery Pass Rd., #190, Mesa, AZ 85207, (480) 984-0032.

White Tank Mountain Regional Park, P.O. Box 91, Waddell, AZ 85355, (623) 935-2505.

Tonto National Forest
Supervisors Office, 2324 E. McDowell Rd., Phoenix, AZ 85006, (602) 225-5200.

Cave Creek Ranger District, 40202 N. Cave Creek Rd., Scottsdale, AZ 85262, (480) 595-3300.

Mesa Ranger District, P.O. Box 5800, Mesa, AZ 85211-5800, (480) 610-3300.

Payson Ranger District, 1009 E. Hwy. 260, Payson, AZ 85541, (520) 474-7900.

Tonto Basin Ranger District, Hwy. 88, HCO 2 Box 4800, Roosevelt, AZ 85545, (520) 467-3200.

Bureau of Land Management
Phoenix Field Office, 2015 W. Deer Valley Rd., Phoenix, AZ 85027, (623) 580-5500.

State of Arizona
Arizona Game and Fish Department, 2221 W. Greenway Rd., Phoenix, AZ 85023-4399, (602) 942-3000.

Arizona State Land Department, 1616 W. Adams St., Phoenix AZ 85007, (602) 542-4625.

US Geological Survey
US Geological Survey, Map Distribution Branch, Box 25286, Denver Federal Center, Denver, CO 80225.

A Short Index of Rides

Doubletrack Cruises
Margies Cove, Sheep Bridge, Doll Baby Ranch, Cypress Thicket, Cottonwood Camp, Rock Creek, Queen Creek, White Canyon.

Doubletrack Workouts
New River West, Devils Hole, Mount Peeley Road, Slate Creek Divide, Four Peaks, El Oso Road, Little Pine Flat, Apache Trail, Woodbury Road.

Sweet Singletrack Rides
Sonoran Loop, Desert Classic Trail, Trail 100, Dynamite Loop, Sport Loop, Long Loop, Pemberton Trail, Blevins Loop, Moon Rock Loop.

Beginner's Luck
Margies Cove, New River Mesa, New River Headwaters, Blevins Loop, Moon Rock Loop, Doll Baby Ranch, Cottonwood Camp, Rock Creek, Queen Creek, White Canyon.

Technical Tests
Technical Loop, Rainbow Valley Loop, Pima Loop, Javelina Loop, New River Loop, Pass Mountain Trail.

Great Climbs—the Yearn to Burn
Humboldt Mountain, Mount Peeley Road, Slate Creek Divide, Four Peaks, El Oso Road.

Glossary

ATB: All-terrain bicycle; a.k.a. mountain bike, sprocket rocket, fat-tire flyer.

ATV: All-terrain vehicle; in this book ATV refers to motorbikes and three- or four- wheelers designed for off-road use.

Bail: Getting off the bike, usually in a hurry, and whether or not you mean to. Often a last resort.

Bunny hop: Leaping up, while riding, and lifting both wheels off the ground to jump over an obstacle (or for sheer joy).

Butt ruff: A rocky trail that pounds the rider through the saddle, especially on descent. Will this term become obsolete with the spread of fully suspended bikes?

Cairn: A pile of stones used to mark a trail.

Chaparral: A mixture of scrub oak, mountain mahogany, and manzanita that forms a thick brush cover in the mountains from about 4,000 to 6,000 feet in central Arizona. Don't try to ride through this stuff!

Clean: To ride without touching a foot (or other body part) to the ground; to ride a tough section successfully.

Contour: A line on a topographic map showing a continuous elevation level over uneven ground. Also a verb indicating a fairly easy or moderate grade: "The trail contours around the west flank of the mountain before the final grunt to the top."

Dab: To put a foot or a hand down (or to hold onto or lean on a tree or other support) while riding. If you have to dab, then you haven't ridden that piece of trail **clean.**

Downfall: Trees that have fallen across the track (also **deadfall**).

Doubletrack: A trail, jeep road, ATV route, or other track with two distinct ribbons of **tread**, typically with grass growing in between. No matter which side you choose, the other rut always looks smoother.

Endo: Lifting the rear wheel off the ground and riding (or abruptly not riding) on the front wheel only. Also known, at various degrees of control and finality, as a nose wheelie, "going over the handlebars," and a face plant.

Fall line: The angle and direction of a slope; the **line** you follow when gravity is in control and you aren't.

Graded: When a gravel road is scraped smooth to level out the washboards and potholes, it has been *graded*. In this book, a road is listed as graded only if it is regularly maintained. Even these roads are not always graded every year.

Granny gear: The innermost and smallest of the chainrings on the bottom bracket spindle (where the pedals and crank arms attach to the bike's frame). Shift down to your granny gear (and up to the biggest cog on the rear hub) to find your lowest ratio for easiest climbing.

Hammer: To ride hard; derived from how it feels afterward: "I'm hammered."

Hammerhead: Someone who actually enjoys feeling hammered; the Type-A rider who goes hard and fast all the time.

Kelly hump: An abrupt mound of dirt across the road or trail. These are common on old logging roads and skidder tracks, placed there to block vehicle access. At high speeds, they become launching pads that transform bikes into satellites and riders into astronauts.

Line: The route (or trajectory) between or over obstacles or through turns. **Tread** or trail refers to the ground you're riding on; the line is the path you choose within the tread (and exists mostly in the eye of the beholder).

Off-the-seat: Moving your butt behind the bike seat and over the rear tire; used for control on extremely steep descents. This position increases braking power, helps prevent **endos**, and reduces skidding.

Pinyon–juniper: A open, dry, pigmy forest of pinyon pine and juniper trees that are usually 10 to 20 feet tall.

Portage: To carry the bike, usually up a steep hill, across unrideable obstacles, or through a stream.

Quads: Thigh muscles (short for quadriceps); or maps in the USGS topographic series (short for quadrangles). The right quads (of either kind) can prevent or get you out of trouble in the backcountry.

Ramada: A roof without walls, constructed to provide shade at picnic areas, campgrounds, and highway rest areas in the desert.

Ratcheting: Also known as backpedaling; pedaling backwards to avoid bashing feet or pedals on rocks or other obstacles.

Sidehill: Where the trail crosses a slope's **fall line**. If the **tread** is narrow, keep your uphill pedal up to avoid hitting the ground. If the tread has a sideways slant, you may have to use body English to keep the bike vertical and avoid side-slipping.

Singletrack: A trail, game run, or other track with only one ribbon of **tread**. Singletrack is pure fun.

SPD: A type of pedal with a binding that accepts a matching cleat on the sole of a bike shoe. The cleat locks to the pedal for more control and efficient pedaling, and is easily un-latched for safe landings (in theory).

Spur: A side road or trail that splits off from the main route.

Surf: Riding through loose gravel or sand, when the wheels slalom from side to side; also *heavy surf*: frequent and difficult obstacles.

Suspension: A bike with front suspension has a shock-absorbing fork or stem. Rear suspension absorbs shock between the rear wheel and frame. A bike with both is said to be fully suspended.

Switchbacks: When a trail goes up a steep slope, it zigzags or *switchbacks* across the **fall line** to ease the gradient of the climb. Well-designed switchbacks make a turn with at least an 8-foot radius and remain fairly level within the turn itself. These are rare, however, and cyclists often struggle through sharply angled, sloping switchbacks.

Tank: A small, seasonal pond with an earthen dam built by ranchers as a water source for cattle.

Track stand: Balancing on a bike in one place, without rolling forward appreciably. Cock the front wheel to one side and bring that pedal up to the one or two o'clock position. Now control your side-to-side balance by applying pressure on the pedals and brakes and changing the angle of the front wheel, as needed. It takes practice but really comes in handy at stoplights, on **switchbacks**, and when trying to free a foot before falling. (See **SPD**.)

Tread: The riding surface, particularly regarding singletrack.

Wash: A desert streambed that is dry most of the time. Washes can flood suddenly, especially during the summer thunderstorm season, and may be running during spring snowmelt.

Water bar: A log, rock, conveyor belting, ditch, or other barrier placed in the **tread** to divert water off the trail and prevent erosion. Peeled logs can be slippery and cause bad falls, especially when they angle sharply across the trail.

Washboard: A rippled surface that develops in heavily used dirt roads. It can usually be avoided on a bike, but if not, it'll rattle your teeth.

About the Author

Bruce Grubbs is an avid hiker, mountain biker, and cross-country skier who has been exploring the American West for over 30 years. An outdoor writer and photographer, he's written 11 other FalconGuides. He lives in Flagstaff, Arizona.